Counselling
in the
New Millennium

A Post Modern Perspective

William J. Kennedy

Detselig Enterprises Ltd.

Calgary, Alberta, Canada

Counselling in the New Millenium
© 1998 William J. Kennedy

Canadian Cataloguing in Publication Data

Kennedy, William J. (William Joseph)
Counselling in the new millenium

Includes bibliographic references
ISBN 1-55059-165-7

1. Counselling.   I. Title.
BF637.C6K46   1998   158'.3   C98-910106-1

Detselig Enterprises Ltd.
210-1220 Kensington Rd. N.W.
Calgary, Alberta T2N 3P5

Detselig Enterprises Ltd. appreciates the financial support for our 1998 publishing program, provided by Canadian Heritage and the Alberta Foundation for the Arts, a beneficiary of the Lottery Fund of the Government of Alberta.

All rights reserved. No part of this book may be reproduced in any form or by any means without permission in writing from the publisher.

Printed in Canada

ISBN 1-55059-165-7

SAN 115-0324

Cover design by Dean Macdonald.

Dedication

To Donna for her constant encouragement and editorial help and to Jason, Aaron and Meghan for their support and patience. Thanks to Tina and Carolyn for giving generously of their time in typing this manuscript.

Table of Contents

Introduction vi

**Chapter 1 – Counselling, Psychotherapy and
Guidance –Similarities and Differences .**   **7**
Counselling Psychology and Counselling   8
Counselling   9
Psychotherapy   12
Guidance   13
Similarities and Differences   14

**Chapter 2 – The Growth and Development
of Counselling** **19**
Counselling in Modern Times   20
Counselling Psychology in Post Modern Times   22
Counselling Psychology Refocused   25
Theoretical Considerations   27

**Chapter 3 – The Counselling Context:
Role and Duties** **31**
Counselling Modes   32
Sharing the Role   35
Needs Identification   37
Assessing Individual Needs and Setting Goals   37
Power Sharing in the Counselling Process   39
Counsellor's Role in Client Career/Job Placement   41
Other Influences that Impact on the
Role of the Counsellor   42
The Counselling Psychologist as Consultant   44
Limitations in Counselling Psychology   46

**Chapter 4 – Personal Qualities of the
Counselling Psychologist** **49**
A Caring Relationship   50
Humor   51

Self-Actualizing Person *53*
Professionalism. *55*

Chapter 5 – Counselling: A Systems Approach **57**
Systems Theory *57*
Counselling from a Systems Perspective *60*

Chapter 6 – Career Counselling in the 21st Century . **69**

Chapter 7 – Career Counselling Young Women . . . **79**
Biases in Career Counselling *85*
Guidelines for Career Counsellors *86*

Chapter 8 – Legal and Ethical Issues in
Counselling Psychology **91**
The Process of Making Ethical Decisions *92*
Confidentiality and Privileged Communication *93*
Informed Consent. *94*
Safety of Clients *97*
Advice Giving *97*
Ethical Issues in Educational Settings *98*
Counselling in the Corporate World *101*
Dual Relationships in Counselling *102*

Chapter 9 – The Counsellor as a
Reflective Practitioner **107**

Chapter 10 – Counselling in Schools: Counsellor/
Teacher/Administrator Relationships . . **117**
Counsellor/Teacher Relationships *117*
Counsellor/Administrator Relationships *120*

References **125**

Introduction

Counselling as a method of helping people has been with us for many centuries. The practice of counselling (helping people) can be traced back to the Greek Philosophers (Fine in Corsini [1973]). However, counselling as we know it and as it is practiced today began its journey towards maturity in the late 19th and early 20th centuries. Its growth and development was influenced by the works of eminent late 19th and early 20th century theorists, practitioners and writers such as Freud, Adler, Jung and Watson. It slowly developed throughout that period and came to the fruition of its present status in the late 1950s and early 1960s, where its growth and development was further nurtured by the writings of Rogers (1951, 1961), May (1958), Skinner (1953), Tyler (1969), Perls (1969), Berne (1967), Ellis (1962) and Frankl (1963). Through these writings and others too numerous to mention, the practice of counselling (psychology) has developed from a "philosophy" which talked about the nature of persons to the more "skill developed practice" that it is today.

More recently, practitioners such as Thorne & Dryden (1993), Eagan (1994), Dryden & Feltham (1992), Culley (1991), Murgatroyd (1985), Dainow and Bailey (1988), Dixon and Glover (1985) and Cottone (1991) and many others, using traditional counselling theories as a basis for their writings, have contributed to the growing counselling knowledge base. The focus in these writings is more on the process of counselling, rather than on the development of new theories. This book utilizes existing counselling theories and practices as a basis for discussing issues which impinge on and influence the day-to-day work of counsellors in the new millennium.

Chapter 1
Counselling, Psychotherapy and Guidance – Similarities and Differences

When asked by Alice what he meant by glory, Humpty Dumpty replied, "a word can mean anything I want it to mean...." (Carroll in Tenniel, 1936, p. 213). This broad, yet personal interpretation of word meaning is as relevant today as it was for Alice in the mid 20th century. In post modern society, meaning is ascribed to words in relation to the "particular" and not in relation to the "universal." Words as symbols are only as meaning specific as the person using them wants them to be in relation to the context in which they apply. The meaning we attribute to words is indeed more "contextual" than "universal" and/or "abstract."

This kind of situational or contextual meaning has been applied to the terms counselling, psychotherapy and guidance. These terms have been defined and differentiated either by the context in which they are carried out and/or by the formal qualifications of the person engaged in their operation. There have been attempts to develop specific definitions of these terms, but as Perry (1961) wrote, thus far, at least, no one has succeeded in defining psychotherapy in a way satisfactory to everyone else. Nor do we know of any definition for counselling (p. 175). Although this statement was made some 36 years ago, it is still applicable today. However, these terms have one common bond, they each describe in their own way certain aspects of the helping professions.

The idea and practice of helping people with problems of a personal and social nature is not a new development and has been practiced in some form or another for quite a long period of time. As the practice of helping grew to professionhood, it became victim to the modernist phenomenon of specialization and hence the need for definition and titles. It has been said that a title is only a "shield behind which weak persons hide" (author unknown). The same can be said for our penchant for definitions. Societies need for titles and/or definitions appears to be a carryover from the positivist era. The positivist's tradition emphasized the rule of scientific precision. This period in history stressed the belief that for something to have meaning it must be capable of the test of experimental, scientific analyses. This emphasis on definition and precision is often summed up in the phrase "Ockham's razor," named after William of Ockham (Boehner, 1957). William, a noted positivist, was pro definition in so far as he believed that things should not be multiplied unnecessarily, but ordered together in some form of scientific, definable bond. In other words, positivists claim that we should include in our world only that which is and/or can be proven or is definable by science or experience. In the positivists' tradition, the notion of giving credence to concepts that are ill defined and/or which encompass ideas that are without foundation in the realm of the scientific, is regarded as useless clutter in a world of experience and scientific realism. Any attempt to put definitions of the helping professions under this kind of rigorous scrutiny would, to say the least, be left lacking. Not only are many of the helping practices that exist under the umbrella of the "helping" professions barely differentiated in their conceptualization, they are only minimally different in their application. In the positivist tradition, differentiated literature regarding these difficult-to-define professions would simply add to the clutter of an already over subscribed body of writings. However, as society moves from the positivist era into post positivist-post modernist thinking, there appears to be a more flexible attitude and belief regarding what constitutes the scientific. Coupled with this attitude is a strong body of belief that science, as defined in modern positivist times, has not been the great savior of our present world, nor has it provided the answer to all our problems (Hargreaves, 1994). However, given these two realities, there is still the need, even in the so-called deconstructed social milieu of the post modern 90s, to have a sense of closure around what we do. We return therefore, to that aspect of positivism, namely, definition of terms, which helps give a sense of closure around the particular profession in which theories are espoused and practiced.

We generally look to definitions not so much for what they can include, but for what they can enable us to exclude. Young (1986) highlights this point when, in referring to the definition of community, he postulates that in the desire to look for an integrated, organic wholeness or community, we cannot help but become involved in a process that inevitably excludes those who do not seem to fit into the community. This exclusionary attribute inherent in the very notion of definition, particularly in the many definitions of professional practice, has driven many practicing in the helping professions to become dogmatic ritualists who find themselves embroiled in a lot of jargonistic gobbledygook. I hope that the following attempt at defining counselling psychology, guidance and psychotherapy will not add to this collage of verbiage but will, at the very least, put some historical perspective on our attempts to make positive sense out of what we do.

Counselling Psychology and Counselling

Counselling Psychology, as a distinct member of the helping professions, is said to have emerged as a separate, unique profession from approximately the early 1950s. According to Wrenn (1966), there were two significant movements during the 50s that gave a sense of identity to the counselling psychology profession, namely, the publication of the *Journal of Counselling Psychology* and the changing of the name of organizations in certain districts of the United States from Counselling and Guidance to Counselling Psychology. Another significant event occurred in September 1951 at a meeting hosted by Gilbert Wrenn under the auspices of the American Psychological Association. At this gathering, according to Super (1955), there was an almost sudden transition from Vocational Guidance to Counselling Psychology. This sense of identity for counselling psychology has been further addressed by Hiebert & Uhlemann (1993). Their research found that respondents identified counselling psychology as a specialization within the broad field of Psychology. The focus of counselling was reported to be working with "normal (versus pathological) clients, living in community (rather than institutional) settings, who are experiencing any number of developmental life issues or personal life crises" (p. 291). Further findings pointed out that "the largest category of concerns . . . included problem areas of unemployment, marital tensions, bereavement, abuse (emotional, physical or substance), stress and anxiety, interpersonal conflicts and chronic illnesses. The second largest category of concerns was preventive. . . . these included adolescents with career concerns, special needs clients, students with low self-esteem" (p. 292).

The events reported by Wrenn and Super and the research reported by Hiebert and Uhlemann and others have added to the literature and given "some" distinction between counselling and counselling psychology. However, at the same time this distinction is not clear or concrete. Most of what has been described (both in content, process and context) as counselling psychology by the respondents to Hieberts and Uhlemanns research can very easily be used in any similar discussion of counselling, with few exceptions, for example, the doctoral rather than masters training usually associated with counselling psychology. Without concrete conclusions regarding a definite distinction between the practice, process and context of counselling and counselling psychology (either in theory or practice) as reported in the literature and given my own belief that the two are synonymous, this book will use the terms counselling and counselling psychology interchangeably.

Counselling

Counselling definitions tend to be similar in content to psychotherapy definitions, and not unlike those of psychotherapy, inexact in conclusion. The American Psychological Association (1956) defines counselling as a process which helps individuals overcome obstacles to their personal growth wherever they may be encountered, and towards achieving optimum use of their personal resources. The emphasis here is on the *personal*. Gustad (1957) puts counselling in the realm of a learning process whereby counsellors help clients learn more about themselves. The aim of this learning process is to help clients define personal goals which will help them become personally fulfilled and hence more productive members of society. Patterson (1959) refers to counselling as the process of giving professional or expert help to persons suffering from full-conscious conflicts which are accompanied by so-called normal anxiety. This definition puts the practice of counselling in realm of conflict resolution with an emphasis on personal growth and development. Again, Parker (1968) picks up this theme of personal growth when he speaks of counselling as the process of restoration and acceleration of growth which is directed towards interpersonal relations, openness and independence. Glanz (1974) follows along this theme of personal growth and learning by putting counselling in the category of an applied social science with an interdisciplinary base which encompasses the fields of psychology, sociology, cultural anthropology, education, economics and philosophy. Glanz believes that each of these disciplines has made, and continues to make, its own unique contribution to counselling. From psychology comes human growth and development, from sociology we adopt the awareness of insight into social structures and institutions, anthropology gives us an understanding of the importance of culture and economics helps in the understanding of the world of work and the importance of career development.

When one looks at why people seek counselling, it becomes obvious how so many professions have influenced its growth. The general overall purpose of counselling is to provide for the optimal development and well being of the individual, while at the same time recognizing that s/he operates and lives in a social context and not in isolation. If the process is to enhance growth and development, then counsellors must be cognizant of the many social factors that impinge on the components of the process. Hence the need for an interdisciplinary bases for the profession (Glanz, 1974).

Jones, cited in Murgatroyd (1985), defines counselling as an enabling process designed to help an individual come to terms with his or her life as it is, and ultimately to grow to greater maturity through learning to take greater responsibility and make decisions for him or herself. Vriend (1985) describes counselling as a process whereby steps are taken to explore what the presenting problem is, to identify and label self-defeating behaviors that feed the problem, to provide insight into the problem and identify alternative behaviors, to make decisions and set goals, and to evaluate the counselling process, that is, to decide what is working and eliminate what is not.

Glosoff & Koprowicz (1990) define counselling as "a process in which a trained professional forms a trusting relationship with a person who needs assistance. This relationship focuses on personal meaning of experiences, feelings, behaviors, alternatives, consequences, and goals. Counselling provides a unique opportunity for individuals to explore and express their ideas and feelings in a non-evaluative, non-threatening environment" (p. 8). Griggs (1994) discusses counseling in the context of learning styles. It is her thesis that we can only be of assistance to people if we understand their particular learning style. When we have established this understanding, we can then embark on a program of counselling that can be tailored to the individual needs of that person.

The above definitions span quite a number of years in the history of counselling. However, they all keep within a common trend, namely, they generally describe counselling as a process that deals with people who require professional help in coming to grips with their personal/social/emotional setbacks, which may or may not be pathological in nature and which are severe enough to prevent a person from getting the most out of life and prevent the person from making a positive contribution to society and the lives of others. These problems can arise from a variety of reasons or sources. They can be intra-personal, for example, low self-esteem, or interpersonal, for example, the inability to form or maintain relationships. They can also be socio-cultural or psycho-social.

Another aspect of counselling that has grown and flourished during the last decade is career counselling. At one time, career counselling was referred to as vocational guidance, but due to socio-economic conditions and the proliferation of literature and research that has come from the pens of scholars during the past ten years, it has taken on a new prominence in the world of counselling. Some question whether this great onslaught of research into career counselling has been politically motivated, that is, whether it was the publishing game of the decade, or if indeed it was motivated by some very serious social vacuum which needed to be filled. Whatever the motivation, counsellor educators and others in the field have developed a literature that quite handily puts career choice and decisions about what to do in life into the realm of the counselling profession (Chapter 6 & 7 deal with this issue at some length). Suffice for our purposes here is to say that career counselling is now an accepted role for the counsellor both in institutions such as schools and hospitals, and in private clinics.

From the above definitions of counselling it would appear that, although there are ranges of variations in the definitions and perceptions of the practice, any differences are more variations on a theme rather than substantive. The definitions show that counselling is concerned with issues that deal with personal growth and development and which are not necessarily, but could be, life threatening. Embodied in the various definitions of counselling are such notions as self-actualization, independence, goal definition, learning styles, emotional instability and interpersonal relationships. The theme that runs through the various definitions is that counselling is concerned with the personal, social, emotional, interpersonal and psychological difficulties that disrupt the process and hinder the development of what has been called normal, psychological/psychosocial growth.

Psychotherapy

Most people from time to time experience a situation where they are helped by some advice from a relative or friend. Perhaps they have made changes in their lives because of new insights gained from talking with others or from reading a book. Alexander (1963) points out that the process of psychotherapy is not too far removed from such common experience. It is his contention that everyone who tries to console a despondent friend or calm down a panicky child, in a sense, practices psychotherapy. S/he uses psychological means in an attempt to restore the disturbed emotional equilibrium of another person. Even these common sense, everyday methods are based on an understanding of the nature of the disturbance. Such an understanding is intuitive rather than scientific. Methodological psychotherapy, to a large degree, is nothing but a systematic, conscious application of methods by which we influence others in our daily lives. What Alexander (1963) is saying here is that the practice of psychotherapy is no more than the ordered application of a helping process that we normally use in our everyday lives when the need arises. Meltzoff and Kornreich (1976), cited in Smith, et al. (1980), define psychotherapy as the informed and planned application of techniques derived from established principles, by persons qualified by training and experience to understand these principles and to apply these techniques, with the intention of assisting individuals to modify such personal characteristics as feelings, values, attitudes and behaviors which are judged by the therapist to be maladaptive or maladjustive (p. 6).

Singer (1965) refers to psychotherapy as a process of making people comprehensive to themselves, to help them fearlessly see themselves and to help them learn that this process of self-recognition, far from producing contempt, implies and brings about the achievement of dignity and fulfillment. In this description the notion of *know thyself* is seen as a positive process and one that will enhance the well-being of the individual. Brammer and Shostrom (1968) speak of psychotherapy as the re-education of the individual with a view to assisting the individual to gain perceptual reorganization, integrating the consequent insights into his/her personality structure and working out methods that handle feelings deep within the personality. This definition brings the practice of education into the therapy and also gives the therapist a very direct role in the process. Fine, cited in Corsini (1973), makes the connection between self-actualization and the process of psychotherapy. Fine's belief is that in the process of psychotherapy we can bring about a sense of personal freedom, which hopefully will maximize the self-actualization potential of the individual. Garner (1970) relates the process of psychotherapy to dealing with those who are mentally sick. Psychotherapy takes place only when a person seeks out a helper because s/he feels sick, physically or mentally, or when such help is sought for the person by others and the helper is a physician with special skills in mental treatment. This definition puts psychotherapy in the medical profession and places the process of care in the realm of a trained physician. Reisman (1971) takes a much simpler view of the process of psychotherapy by defining it as the communication of person-related understanding and a wish to be of help.

In general, the above definitions suggest that the aims of the practice of psychotherapy are to bring about changes in some maladaptive behaviors experienced by individuals, to help change environmental conditions that may impact negatively on these behaviors, to improve interpersonal skills, to alleviate personal stress, to help people form positive assumptions about themselves and their world and to help people form a true sense of identity. These definitions offer a wide range of practices from assisting people to reach their maximum personal potential, to assisting the so-called mentally sick. Definitions of psychotherapy appear to be based on the notion that psychological, sociological and biological factors play a role in mental disorders. It works from the premise that even in cases where physical pathology is present, the individual's perceptions, expectations and coping strategies play a role in the development of the disorder and will probably need to be changed or adjusted if recovery is to take place. It can be said that the underlying tenet of the practice of psychotherapy is that psychological problems can be elevated or eliminated if a person can learn more adaptive ways of perceiving, evaluating and behaving.

Guidance

During the late 50s and early 60s, the term guidance became prominent in describing another practice in the helping professions. This practice dates back to the early 1900s and is linked to the work of Parsons (1908) who established around that time the Vocational Bureau of Boston. From there the movement grew. In 1951, The American Personnel and Guidance Association was founded and in 1959, a similar organization The Canadian Guidance and Counselling Association was formed in Canada. Although guidance began as a vocational placement movement, it quickly became an integral part of the school system and took on responsibility for a whole range of activities that dealt with all aspects of the life of the student. The following definitions will give only a cursory look at attempts to define the "guidance movement" which reached its apex during the 1960s and 1970s.

Hoyt (1962) clearly places the practice of guidance within the school system. He regards the guidance person as the key individual in that institution who, with others such as teachers, is responsible for the personal needs of the students. Jones (1963) defines guidance as assisting people and enabling them to develop the ability to make intelligent choices and adjustments. Guidance, according to Jones, does not make choices for people but helps them make their own. In so doing, it stimulates the gradual development of the person to make decisions independently. Guidance aims at aiding the individual to grow to independence and responsibility for self. According to Jones, guidance is an integral part of the educative process and its centre is clearly there. Blocher, Dustin and Dugan (1971) also describe guidance as that which ensures a comprehensive program of educational experience. They contend that guidance is concerned with the development of the whole person within the educational setting.

Although these definitions seem to put a very positive spin on the guidance movement as a separate profession, other writers were not as convinced of its merits. They questioned whether there was a need at all for the practice and if, indeed, the addition of the title as a prefix to counselling (Guidance Counselling) was misleading. McCully (1962), for example, argues that the term guidance ought to be abandoned because it actually referred to a point of view and activities that are not necessarily the special province of the school counsellor. McCully suggests that to tag one person with the guidance of students would seem to make the person indistinguishable from other persons in the school, for example, teachers who could lay equal claim to exposing the guidance point of view.

Guidance definitions, like those of counselling and psychotherapy, put it in the realm of the helping professions. Like counselling and psychotherapy, guidance is considered to address, at least to some degree, issues related to the personal growth and social development of the individual. However, unlike counselling and psychotherapy, it is placed in a specific context, namely, education and more specifically, the school. It refers to a specific population, namely, school students, and deals specifically with difficulties which are more academic in nature.

Similarities and Differences

These historic and current definitions of the three terms, counselling and psychotherapy and guidance, present some general similarities and differences. The one common element they have is that they are all listed under the general heading of helping professions. Guidance is different from both counselling and psychotherapy in so far as it is designated to help a specific group of clients, namely students. Its focus is to help students with their educational needs and to assist them to get the most out of the educative process. When guidance is looked at in this way, it is not necessarily within the domain of any one individual in the school setting. Helping students get the most out of their educative process is indeed the raison d'être of all the professionals in the school setting, which include the principal, teachers, etc., and therefore cannot be designated to one individual. It can also be argued that many so-called guidance counsellors in schools today are no longer engaged directly in the personal/social/emotional lives of the students. Instead, they spend most, if not all of their time, involved in developing time table schedules, helping students select courses and job placement. It can be argued that this worthwhile, yet non-counselling function can as easily be done by an understanding and knowledgeable non-academic. A person does not necessarily need graduate work in counselling to fulfil this function. One could become competent in this area with a concentration in many different fields of study, for example, administration, teaching or curriculum. Also, in present teacher education programs, teaching is seen as more than instructing in a specific subject. Teacher education programs today purport a philosophy that deals with the concept of holistic education. That is to say, every attempt is made in teacher education programs to emphasize teaching as a guidance as well as an academic process. This philosophy emphasizes the need for teachers to be aware, not only of the students need to learn, but also their need to know why they are learning and what personal and social circumstances impact on this learning. Teaching includes helping students choose the proper curriculum that will lead them to successful completion of their academic programs. Teaching today embodies all that guidance purports to hold, namely, helping students pass successfully through the school curriculum. This does not in any way imply that there is not a need in schools for a person specially trained as a counsellor. Indeed, it highlights the role of the school counsellor as defined in this book and puts the work of the counsellor where it belongs, namely, in the realm of helping students cope with their social, emotional, intra- and interpersonal difficulties, which impinge negatively on their lives as persons, as well as students. The distinct role and need for counselling will be evident throughout the following chapters.

Rogers (1942), in addressing the issue of differences between the processes of counselling and psychotherapy, considered the differences to be insubstantial. Although he does admit that there may be some reasons for the distinction between the two, he suggests that intensive and successful counselling is indistinguishable from intensive and successful psychotherapy. Hahn & Maclean (1955) agree with Rogers that there is a lot of similarity between counselling and psychotherapy. However, they differentiate between the two on the bases of context. Hahn & Maclean contend that there are indeed no deep-seated conflicts of interest between the counsellor and the psychotherapist. However, they contend that, although counselling and psychotherapy share a common rich background in training, they tend to operate in quite different settings with different clients. However, Tyler (1958) sees a definite division between counselling and psychotherapy, especially in terms of their specific aims. According to Tyler, psychotherapy deals with personality change whereas counselling deals with helping clients utilize their resources to their fullest potential. Blum and Bolinsky (1962) disagree with Tyler. They contend that counselling might be considered synonymous with therapy if the latter is to be considered a process fostering individual growth, so that they can handle problems that they formerly could not. Arbuckle (1965) again does not make any distinction between counselling and psychotherapy. He contends that the competent, professionally educated counsellor is involved in all the human relationships that have been described by various individuals as either counselling or psychotherapy. Patterson (1966) sees no essential difference between the two either in process, the nature of the relationship, the methods or techniques or in goals or outcomes. Vance & Volsky (1962) make a distinction between counselling and psychotherapy based on the notion that counselling deals with non-pathological issues whereas psychotherapy deals with both pathological and non-pathological issues. For them any differences in counselling and psychotherapy can best be understood not by specialty designation but by process. Vance & Volsky contend that in counselling the processes deal with many factors not necessarily pathological. Psychotherapy processes, on the other hand, deal with the pathological and aim to cure. Blocher (1966) suggests that it is better to deal with the differences by looking at their goals rather than their methodologies. It is his belief that the goals of counselling are developmental, educative and preventive, and the goals of psychotherapy are remedial, adjustive and therapeutic. Brammer and Shostrum (1968) also use goals as a differentiating method between the two practices. Their list of goals is similar to Blocher's. They list the goals of counselling to be educative, supportive, situational, problem solving, and with an emphasis on the "normal." Their goals for psychotherapy are supportive, reconstructive with a depth emphasis, focus on the unconscious, with an emphasis on neuroses or severe emotional difficulties. Steffler & Grant (1972) appear to be using context as a differentiating point when they suggest that psychotherapists are more apt to work in hospital or private settings while counsellors are more apt to work in educational and/or community settings. However, given the type of designated setting, they appear to be agreeing with the kinds of differences outlined by Brammer and Shostrum (1968) and Blocher (1966).

It can be said that the above definitions and comparisons outline some of the similarities and differences that have and do exist in the practices of helping others through counselling, guidance and psychotherapy. Views on differentiation and similarities of three different practices of the helping professions have been presented. It has been noted that when discussing the helping professions, the term guidance fits well into the educative process and belongs within the domains of "all" educators in the school. The practice of guidance, which was mostly confined to the schools, is no longer seen as a specialty and the domain of just one person. Indeed, when one looks at the definition of teaching as expounded in the literature today, one can see many similarities between the teacher as teacher and the teacher as guidance person (Cooper et al., 1994). The two work descriptions appear to be synonymous. It is the professional duty of all who work in the school system to be aware of the educative problems and needs of the students in the school and how these impact on their future education.

Counselling and psychotherapy, on the other hand, are terms that are as strong and vibrant today as they have been for many years. As the reader will notice, the definitions of counselling and psychotherapy put forth here for the most part are not recently coined but come from a literature of past decades. There is a paucity of literature today that discusses specifically their differences or similarities. Popular literature would seem to suggest that the two terms are used interchangeably. There also appears to be a move away from the term 'psycho' therapy towards the use of therapy alone, or indeed the use of "counselling" as a generic and interchangeable term to describe the general process of helping.

There are some who work in the helping professions today who have little or no concern if they are referred to as a therapist, psychotherapist or counsellor. They regard the titles of counsellor or psychotherapist as merely walls which afford personal/professional protection and which engender in the clients a belief that within this title lies a "knowledgeable person" who is capable of helping them. These professionals reflect the openness of post modern society. They are more holistic in their outlook and more systems oriented. However, other professionals still cling tenaciously to their modernist labels and refuse to see the folly of such meaningless distinctions. Therefore, it becomes necessary occasionally to make some statement regarding these issues. I hope that this chapter will engender some discussion and that it will give some credence to the need for debate regarding the use of labels in general and the real or perceived differences that exist among various helping professions. Hopefully this discussion will not only bring about more understanding between the three practices but will also result in a more integrative and holistic systemic relationship within all of the helping professions.

Chapter 2
The Growth and Development of Counselling

"Helping" people in terms of their emotional and psychological well-being is not a new concept. It can be traced from the time of the Greek and Roman philosophers (Fine in Corsini, 1973), through the modern era of the 19th and early 20th centuries to the post modern era of the present. Helping people through the use of psycho-social intervention, or what we call today counselling, has gone through continual growth and development, especially during the period from the mid 1950s to the 1980s, known as the post modern era (Rosenau, 1992; Jencks, 1987). Throughout this growth counselling has had difficulty in establishing its own unique identity, Whiteley (1980), Whitelet & Fretz (1980), Zytowski & Rosen (1982). However, this "identity crisis" seems to have abated and the profession appears to have matured and stabilized. Recent writings such as those of Dryden (1991), Eagan (1994), Culley (1991) and Cottone (1991) appear to be more like variations on a theme rather than new discoveries or further development of new theoretical platforms. Counselling has now established itself and claims its own professional identity and status.

This extensive growth of counselling, both as a profession and as a consumer commodity, has been largely due to the increasing need felt by the members of the community at large for help in understanding and making sense of their lives. Counselling psychology has become an established integral part of our society and has in many ways touched at least some aspects of the lives of all of us. Counselling has received, or at least has been given, such prominence in postmodern times because it is a tool that can be used by many people as a kind of psycho-social prop to help them survive in what is perceived by them to be an uncertain society. This need has been fostered by such factors in our society as affluence, concomitant with excessive consumerism, coupled with a shrinking value of currency. Counselling in post modern times has become for many a "filler" for the vacuum caused by the breakdown of social interaction/relations and traditional institutions such as family, churches, schools, etc., within society. This perceived lack of social connectedness and concomitant personal isolation in a shrinking globalized society is no doubt one of the great paradoxes of present day post modern society. Counselling has filled the void of social interaction for many in a world where, as Marx (1984) predicted, virtue, love, conviction, knowledge, conscience, etc. is passed into commerce. This comment is seen played out in the fact that society today is willing to pay for some form of social interaction when it experiences difficulties which, for the most part in the past, were solved within the context of family or friends.

There are many factors that have impacted on counselling and influenced its growth, development and direction. Many of these factors are due to or are the result of changes and influences associated with the modern and post modern era. Indeed, it was during these periods that counselling experienced its most rapid growth and development. Because of their impact on the development of counselling psychology, I feel that some discussion of the changes and influences of the modern and post modern eras is appropriate.

Counselling in Modern Times

Modernism was the dominant social philosophy until circa 1950 (Duska, 1993). During the early years of modernism, society was perceived as a place where what we did and what we thought were stable and clearly categorized. Like the great Caesar's camp, there was a place for everything and everything was in its place. There was a feeling of order and certitude about the evolving social structure and generally there was no perceived need for counselling services on any wide scale basis. However, as the period of modernism progressed, and the order and stability of the social order in society weakened, a sense of insecurity resulted. This led society to search for an understanding of this new evolving social climate and consequently a need for a better understanding of the psyche or the inner person emerged. This change in social structure also gave rise to a need to re-establish one's place within it. To some extent, it can be said that the roots of our present day "helping" professions are found in these social developments and further expanded over the next hundred years in the writings of Spencer (1860), Freud (1920) and Fromm (1947).

During the mid 19th century, there occurred a great upsurge of interest in the human person, especially in relation to personal inner growth and development. The writings of Spencer (1860), although strongly influenced by the economics and politics of the time, gives a picture of the growing interest in humanity and its development in light of its "expanding" and "free" nature. In the early 20th century, Freud, the father of psychoanalysis, moved our understanding or at least our curiosity about the human psyche from that of scepticism to one of understanding and helping. Fromm (1947) added another page in the development of the helping professions by introducing the notion of human values into the theory of dealing with healthy psychological development. Fromm believed that the value judgments we make determine our actions, and upon their validity rests our mental health and happiness. Fromm believed that neurosis, for example, is itself in the last analysis a symptom of moral failure, although adjustment is by no means a symptom of moral achievement. A major landmark in the development of what we know today as the helping professions was the opening of a psychological laboratory by Wundt in 1879 at the University of Leipzig in Germany.

Later in the period of modernism, the writings of Szasz (1960) and Mower (1960) equate moral values with mental illness. Szasz (1960) rejected the reality of mental illness and hence the need for the so-called helping professions. However, he agrees with Fromm's idea of the interconnectedness of moral values and personal malaise. Szasz (1960) argued that mental illness was a myth whose function is to disguise and thus render more palatable the bitter pill of moral conflict in human relations. Mower (1960) similarly concerned with moral issues and mental illness, described mental symptoms as reflections of unacknowledged, unavowed and unexpiated sin and resultant guilt. Szasz (1960), Mower (1960) and Fromm (1947) seem to suggest the process of helping others is to a large extent influenced by society's particular belief system regarding what are acceptable basic human moral values. Thus moral values were given prominence in the quest for meaning and understanding of the human psyche. Our personal-social value system then becomes intricately entwined in our quest for meaning and self-understanding. This search to give meaning to the psyche through our value system is evident throughout the development of the existential and humanist therapies and is supported in the writings of Frankl (1963), Rogers (1951, 1961) and Satir (1972).

The quest to find meaning to life was further expanded by Maslow's (1968) theory of human needs. Maslow contended that the meaning of life was concomitant with another value of the human condition, namely, the need to be self-fulfilled. In order for this value to be realized, it requires the fulfillment of some basic needs. Maslow (1970) outlined, in hierarchical order, what he believed to be the basic human requirements for our physical and psychological survival and fulfillment. At the bottom of this hierarchy are the basic physiological needs for such items as clothing, shelter, economic security, etc. At the higher levels are placed the intellectual/aesthetic needs fulfillment and at the top of the pyramid is the ultimate fulfillment of "self-actualization." Maslow's paradigm of needs is very much in keeping with the human potential movement of the 70s when people came to the realization that the fulfillment of physiological needs was not sufficient in itself for what had become known then as true "self-actualization." The post-war materialism, although embraced by most as positive, was also seen by many to be lacking in personal fulfillment. People were becoming cynical about pure materialism and the search was focused on the development of their personal, emotional, social and spiritual potential. There was the belief that because material wealth abounded, there was no need to worry about the fulfillment of our basic needs. The current thinking of the time was that one had to move beyond preoccupation with these more basic needs towards fulfilling higher needs. The perceived affluence indicated that there was less time needed for basic need fulfillment and thus more time available for searching for self-development in the areas of the emotional, intellectual and the more hedonistic values of pleasure and play.

Other developments have impacted on the growth of counselling psychology and, indeed, on all of the "helping" professions in the modern era. The growth and development of the disciplines of child and adolescent psychology in the early 1900s, the psychological testing movement which was growing at the same time, and more recently the rapid increase in the theory and practice of family counselling have all contributed in no small measure to the need for and hence the rapid growth of counselling during the modern era. They continue to be a force in its growth and like a gentle wind they continue to influence its development into the post modern era.

Counselling Psychology in Post Modern Times

The sense of security and certainty in values and social structures enjoyed in the modern era was badly shaken with the advent of the post modern period. Society was perceived as moving away from the philosophy of positivism. Belief systems and social values were and continue to be seen as less certain and more particularized or individualistic.

The post modern era – which some say has its early development dated to the 1950s, Duska (1993) and others to the mid 1960s (Ferry and Renaut, 1990) – has been described in the literature in many ways. Generally, the period has been defined by writers such as Lyotard (1984), Hargreaves (1994), Gergen (1990) and Giroux (1988) as a philosophy or belief system that challenges the presence of a single meta-narrative and substitutes instead a belief in the reality of multiple-narratives. In other words, it is an era where individuals are looking for, not one, but many authentic voices. Post modernism challenges the values of well established systems (church, state, family) in a time of globalization of economics and education, and instant world communication. It is an era where once-held-unquestioned disciplines, such as science, are no longer seen as the only and certain source of answers to a better life (Rosenau, 1992). Post modernism questions, for example, the once firmly-held economic theories and seeks to replace them. In the post modern philosophy, traditional knowledge and one time impermeable moral truths appear to have lost much of their credibility. Post modernism has been described as a "particular social condition, a historical juncture that is said to capture the fractured world in which we now live" (Beyer & Liston, 1992, p. 372). Post modernism, with its weakening of belief and confidence in a meta-belief system, coupled with the reality of instant personal contact via the electronic highway, has brought with it changes in our personal life values. It has also heightened our awareness of cultural differences and changed our relationship with peoples of other nationalities. One might say that post modernism has resulted from, or maybe has been the cause of, these changing societal values, globalization of education and economics, and the development of cyber space.

The post modern era has not only forced us to look at changes in the social order, but has challenged us personally to look at the way we see ourselves. Post modernism has challenged us to become aware of these changes in terms of how they impact on us as individuals and as a society. Since these changes are reflected in relation to ourselves and our own personal growth, and in our relationships with others, we are forced to question who we are and who/what we are becoming. Personal anxiety is thus increased as we search for our real self and national identities. This questioning and searching is made more difficult without the security and certitude of the moral tenets of the modernist era and without a firm grounding in the context of some certitude regarding our socio-political and economic reality in the present, and our status within the global techno-rational society of the future (Hargreaves, 1994; Gergen, 1990).

At the inception of the post modern era, a great sense of personal freedom and individualism, and an attitude of nonconformity swept the western world. The economy was booming. People could now put their emphasis on striving for the higher needs of self-actualization and were no longer compelled to spend their day-to-day lives solely providing their basic needs. It was during the 1960s and 70s, a period which emphasized individualism (and some would say narcissism), that a number of significant counselling psychology theories such as those of Perls (1969), Berne (1967), Rogers (1961) and Maslow (1968), were developed and published. These theorists were influenced by the tide of individualism that was prevalent in society and their writings reflect this philosophy. "Personal growth" became the dominant social theme and underscored most of the psychological theories. However, Maslow's (1968, 1970) self-actualization theory, based on a developmental approach to personal needs fulfillment through progressive developmental stages, was a most influential force. Maslow's theory, coupled with the humanistic theory of Rogers (1951, 1961), led to a virtual growth industry in human potential development. Consequently, in their quest for self-actualization, individuals demanded from society some psycho-social assistance to help them make positive progress as they developed (grew) through their developmental stages. This search for self-actualization required a process to make it happen. This led to a rapid growth in counselling psychology, which was perceived to be capable of providing this assistance.

The search for personal fulfillment and the desire for self-actualization and personal needs gratification continued into the 80s. Belief in the traditional institutions of church, state and family were gradually weakened or at least modified to the point where they were no longer seen to be acceptable sources of help and understanding in the search for personal growth or need fulfillment. Counselling psychology continued to rise in popularity and prominence as a substitute for these institutions and was used more and more by society as a helping vehicle in coming to grips with many of life's developmental difficulties. Counselling psychology was seen as "the" channel whereby an individual could attain fulfillment and personal happiness. Counselling became readily available, especially to young people in institutions such as schools, colleges and universities, but was also taking its place in the work force and the community in general. It was accepted by youth in particular as a non-judgmental, person-centred helping process which would get them through their "normal" day-to-day personal problems and difficulties and lead them towards self-actualization. Counselling psychology thus became an accepted, sought-after psychological process in solving problems and fulfilling the needs of "all" people who thought they needed it. Its scope of helping was extended beyond what it was in earlier times. Counselling psychology grew from a process of helping people "in need," to a process of offering help to all "ordinary or normal" people who wished to become self-fulfilled and self-actualized in their day-to-day lives.

The development of counselling has been further influenced by some of the paradoxes inherent in the post modern era. For example, in the 60s and 70s, individual differences were highlighted, yet social and group interaction were preached and practiced. Peace and love movements flourished amidst the shocking horror of the Vietnam War. In the 80s and 90s, technology enhanced our knowledge and understanding of self and others. However, at the same time, it caused us to be almost in a constant state of mistrust and inter/intrapersonal instability. Never have we as a society been perceived as being so accessible and open, that is, globalized, yet as individuals, we act closed, introspective and nationalistic. The collapse of the "communist block" in the last decade has led to the end of the fear of global destruction by the super-powers. However, the fallout from this breakup has lead to a proliferation of smaller but fiercely nationalistically-driven nations. These nations, although small both geographically and in population, are in themselves creating a sense of chaos and uncertainty. They are searching for voices which had been silenced too long by the promoters of the grand-narrative of such ideologies as communism and they are now attempting to rediscover an identity which had been smothered by imposed ideologies other than their own. Another paradox of post modernism has been the implementation by governments of what has been called rational economics, deregulation and a free market frenzy. Although this kind of economic policy may have brought a positive result to the economic recession, it has also resulted in the creation of a new "underclass" of working poor or unemployed people, while at the same time adding prosperity to an already wealthy upper-class. These paradoxes and changes to the structure and essence of society brought about by (during) post modernism have had broad implications for the present day practice of the counselling psychology profession.

Counselling Psychology Refocused

Counselling Psychology, which blossomed as a source of psychosocial help for society in its drive towards self-actualization in the 60s and 70s, was presented with a different challenge in the late 80s and 90s. Economic Rationalism replaced Keynesian economic theory. This fundamental shift in economic policy, with its emphasis on private sector-trickle down-economy, left many who were socio-economically sufficient in the old world order (late modernism and early post modernism) alone and out of work. A new class of educated unemployed, and indeed a new underclass, was rapidly developing. The economic boom of the 60s and 70s was ending and recession replaced self-actualization as the new buzz word. Different needs emerged in society as the economy radically changed from "boom" to "gloom." Consequently, the emphasis for counselling psychology also radically changed.

In addition to these economic changes, institutions such as churches, schools and family had not returned to the place of relevance or reverence that they had enjoyed in the modernist era. People now had more individual freedoms, and indeed, opportunities for more global interpersonal openness had become possible. However, at the same time, despite the long search for self-actualization concomitant with economic security, the economic turnaround had left many individuals to wander alone and aimless.

To some extent, Maslow's theory of self-actualization by the fulfillment of needs through a hierarchical process was proven to be not easily realized. The theory was, and still is, a helpful and worthy concept. Like all theoretical concepts, however, to be lasting it had to stand the test of practical application. In practice, Maslow's theory had fallen short of its expectations. Financial need, which had been taken for granted in the search for the higher psychological needs in the previous two decades, had once again raised its ugly head. The search for fulfillment of higher human needs, that is, actualization, was easily superseded by economic needs and was put on hold. Once again, as in the 40s and 50s, society had returned to search for the fulfillment of a more basic need, that of economic survival.

The forced return to the emphasis on fulfilling "basic" needs coupled with the quest for economic survival and work opportunity, had become and continues to be a basic bench mark in the search for fulfillment and meaning in the post modern society of the 1990s. This quest after economic security (fulfillment) is not new and can be linked back to at least the period of the industrial revolution. However, society in late modern times had adopted a consumer materialism mentality unheard of in early and pre modern times, which emphasized work, wealth and position in the work place as crucial to a strong identity. Disproportionate growth in the value of this materialism, combined with the rapid growth in technology and its consequent impact on the job market, reduced many previously "successful" consumers into a position of seeking for simple survival. This change has impacted heavily on counselling psychology. Consequently, a major focus of counselling psychology today is on the nature and development of the work and economic environment and their consequent impact on the individual. The search for individual personal development is very much part of our present day world as it was two decades ago. However, the individual is now more concerned about his/her place in society and where he/she fits into a world, which is not at all like the world that was to be, or at least was perceived to have been built during the 60s and 70s.

Today, individuals are still looking for meaning in their lives but are seeing the reality of where this meaning lies through very different lenses than during the past decades. Individuals today continue to look for "meaning" which they thought they had, or at least could have found in the 70s and 80s, but are now left with a feeling of disillusionment. The helping professions today are trying to assist people to disentangle themselves from the many paradoxes and contradictions of the post modern era. The objectives of counselling have to include a process to help clients come to some meaningful understanding and acceptance of themselves and of a society that was "not supposed to be" and where freedom of choice seems almost untenable. Counselling psychology in the post modern era, therefore, is challenged to help people come to grips with the feeling of loss of socio-political and economic security, which were taken for granted in the modern world, and also to help individuals work through the paradoxes and contradictions of the post modern world. Counselling is now challenged to assist people who are attempting to come to some meaningful understanding and acceptance of themselves in a society that was "not supposed to happen." In a sense, in the search for actualized selves during the 1970s and 1980s, we had not "found ourselves," as much as we had "found ourselves wanting."

Post modernism, with its different societal conditions and uncertainties, which are exacerbated by economic need and destabilization of traditional icons, demands a different focus from counselling. The need for society to come to grips with this new reality of "economic instability" and "identity crisis" further enhances the need, albeit differently from previous decades, for counselling psychology services. As the social context in which counselling is practiced has changed over the past two decades, the demands on the profession have become somewhat different as well. Counselling psychologists today continue to provide their clients with counselling similar to traditional practices, that emphasize intra- and interpersonal enhancement. However, due to a sense of need by clients to be grounded in the context of some reality in this so-called time-compressed society (Hargreaves 1994), counselling has been forced to shift its emphasis somewhat to fit the demands by clients for quick fixes and here and now solutions. Clients today can no longer, or at least feel they can no longer, go through the slow growth towards self-actualization. The economically-driven needs of the post modern world demand here and now solutions. In the absence of the grand theory of fulfillment and hedonistic bliss of the 60s and 70s, clients in the 90s want to learn from counsellors how to cope with loneliness, stress, job loss and re-entry into a ever-changing job market. Clients are demanding from counsellors immediate solutions to cope with the technological demands which are impacting on their personal/social systems, their career and educational decision making. There is a demand for more crisis management sessions as clients struggle with reintegration into what presents itself to them as an "unknown" society. Clients are struggling with the fallout from their loss of family and community network systems. They want all of these services coupled with a quick dose of positive coping skills. To help this refocusing of counselling practice to occur, it is necessary to revisit counselling theory.

Theoretical Considerations

As previously indicated, counselling theory used today largely grew out of the modernist era. Consequently, it is constructed on the belief in a meta-narrative and based on predictability and order. Many clients who seek counselling today, on the other hand, have grown up in the late modern and post modern era. Their belief systems are situated not in one, but in many authentic voices. They live in a world of uncertainty, instability and, some would argue, chaos. Clients in the post modern globalized world have different needs, wants and beliefs. They come from many and varied backgrounds with their own very different personal practical theories (Handal & Lauvas, 1987). The different needs of clients in the post modern context have implications for the counselling psychologist and should be reflected in both counselling practice and theory.

To meet the demands of clients in the post modern era, counselling psychology theory should not come from some dated or stagnant meta-narrative. Instead theory should develop from an eclectic, contextual, dynamic and affective basis (Gergen, 1992). The meta-narratives of the past no longer fit the present. This necessitates the need for counselling psychology theories to be seen as coming from, and having some "context" base. Within this context, theories have to be dynamic and be able to question without intimidation, the many and varied issues which they encounter. Theories must be developed with an awareness of the emotional (feeling) as well as the cognitive/productive (practical) side of humanity (Gergen, 1992). That is to say that theories need to reflect the "whole" person seen in the context of his/her society. Only in this sense will theory be of help to counsellors in their attempts to make personal sense of their lives and the lives of their clients.

Counselling psychologists need to develop for themselves a theoretical basis for their counselling framed within an understanding of the social ethos and milieu of the present day realities. In order to develop an effective counselling practice, counselling psychologists must have a sound personal counselling theory. Brammer and Shostrum (1968) suggest that a counsellor who does not have a solid foundation in the current thinking and research in the field, as well as a solid counselling philosophy, is only using "cookbook techniques," that is, oversimplified imitations, to help clients with their problems. This advice is as valid today as it was in the 70s. In developing theory, it should be remembered by counselling psychologists that theories are only social connectors. They are the linkage between the cognitive musings of the theorist and present day social realities. On the one hand, in post modern society, there is the deconstructed, hence volatile, knowledge base from which or on which the theory is built and from which it emanates. On the other hand, and I feel more importantly, is the theory's ability to reflect today's social realities and to be understood and communicated to others (Hassard, 1996).

As workers in the helping professions of the post modern era, counsellors must decide how their theory fits into their own present counselling belief system and counselling practice. They must critically analyze their personal theories and the basic assumptions that underpin them. In this way they can develop theories and techniques that are in sync with present day contexts. Counselling psychologists must be able to deconstruct their old theories and reconstruct out of these alternative ones that reflect the existing world in which their clients live and work. Placing their theory in context should heighten counsellors' awareness of the need to conceptualize and recognize in practice the totality of the client's social milieu.

Theory and practice share a symbiotic relationship. Therefore, theory must go beyond mere description and provide a basis for a meaningful plan of action and also give a sense and reflective meaning to their (the counsellors') day-to-day practice in the work place (Hansen, Stevic & Warner, 1986; Brammer & Shostrum, 1968). Gergen (1992) places theory in the context of that which gives cultural meaning to the worker. His thesis is that theory cannot be evaluated solely by its "capacity to predict, for in themselves theories are only sounds or markings, lifeless and inert words that do not predict. Theory gets its importance from acts *practice* (my emphasis) which it enables. This essentially means that theory gets its significance through ongoing patterns of relationships" (p. 210). Theorists merely bring to readable print or popular discussion ideas that actually echo what is important or popular in an existing culture. These ideas/concepts, if accepted by the masses, generate some new forms or ways of acting or behaving. This process thus enables people to actuate their particular cultural belief systems in ways that are more meaningful for them (p. 210). I believe that what Gergen (1992) is saying is that theory does not come from some pure state of thinking, but is merely a sounding out of some underlying belief system of an already existing cultural-social thought, or in some cases, reality.

Theories are the "what ifs" of the inquisitive mind. They become rejected or accepted on the basis of whether they fit or do not fit into the individual's and societies' particular belief systems. For example, behaviorism as a theoretical basis for counselling psychology was adopted and defended by those whose personal beliefs were similar to the tenets which it upheld. Similarly, the humanistic approach to counselling was accepted by those who had a different view than the behaviorists of what constituted the driving forces of human behavior. The point is that neither of these particular theories was the so-called grand-theory or meta-theory that held "all" the answers for "all" those engaged in the practice of counselling psychology. They did, however, reflect the beliefs that a large portion of the population held regarding the socio-cultural ambiance or ethos of the time.

In the "modernist" period, there were many who believed that these theories did represent the grand-narrative and that they held the keys to unlocking the mysteries of the human psyche. The theorists of the modernist era held that a particular counselling theory which they adopted was immutable and fixed and all-embracing. Consequently, practices that emanated from these perceived omniscient theories were also accepted as cure-alls and infallible. Any deviations from these fixed theoretical stances were seen as just that, simply deviations. The theorist of the post modern era cannot make such assumptions. The theorist of the post modern era needs to regard theories as mutable and fallible, with a built in penchant to change. Like science and technology, theories in post modern society are not immutable and infinite but malleable and finite. The post modern theorist lives with a belief in the "reality of the absence" of the meta-narrative or grand-theory and accepts the presence of many mini-narratives and personal theories that in themselves give meaning to life.

Frankl's (1969) *The Will to Meaning* supports the belief in the necessity of giving personal meaning to theoretical development and makes personal meaning important to live a fulfilling life. It holds that it is the will of the individual that gives meaning to life, not the will of the state or some other ordained grand organization. This theoretical stance is represented in the post modern world in so far as the post modern world represents a shift from the objective (the meta-narrative) to the subjective, that is, the voice of the individual (Lyotard, 1993). Counselling psychology theories in the post modern era need to address and reflect on the particular belief systems and socio-cultural realities of the present before they can claim to represent the voices of the community which they serve.

The development of counselling psychology as a literature-based profession has been long and interesting. As a profession, it has, and continues to be, influenced by the socio-cultural milieu of the times. For this reason it is imperative that counselling theory reflect current social demands. Whatever the theoretical perspective from which the counsellor may come, the general underpinnings of counselling theory should have some reality context. The fact that counselling responds to the needs of a particular societal demand at a particular time is indeed one of the reasons that it continues to grow and develop, both in theory, practice and research. It matters not whether counselling psychologists are adherents of any particular theory. Whether they are Jungian, Rogerian, Freudian or indeed eclectic is not the question. What matters is that they are able to see and interpret any counselling theory in today's context. By placing theory in some here and now context, counsellors can develop for themselves a sound theoretical position with a historical as well as a current basis. Counselling from the underpinnings of this combined theoretical structure will enable the counsellor to carry out a practice which will help clients develop confidence both within themselves and their society, establish a secure contextual foundation, and help clients function within that context with self-confidence, pride and a strong personal/social identity.

Chapter 3
The Counselling Context: Role and Duties

Just as the post modern social milieu has, and continues to impact on the interpretation of counselling theories, it also influences the counselling modes or ways of practicing counselling psychology. Although this impact has precipitated changes in the role of counsellors and influenced their practice, many basic counselling practices remain unchanged. This chapter will explore and comment on some of the roles and duties of the counsellor in present day practice.

Much has been written on the role of the counsellor (Griggs, 1994; Culley, 1991; Vriend, 1985; Tyler, 1969). Although to some extent role is defined by the environment in which counsellors work, there are, however, certain duties which are common to almost all counsellors. It is presumed that counsellors in any situation, private or institutional, will be responsible for directly counselling clients on matters of personal positive growth, self-understanding/ actualization, career planning and positive decision making. To enable counsellors to best carry out this primary duty, they should be as free as possible from any administrative and/or clerical assignments which could interfere with their responsibilities as a professional counsellor. Their priority is to help clients establish practices that will help them become self-sufficient in their own lives and a productive member of society (Ligon & McDaniel, 1970).

The specific type of counselling which an aspiring counsellor decides to pursue will, to a large degree, depend on his or her particular theoretical orientation, e.g., cognitive, behaviouristic, humanistic, etc. However, in working with clients it is believed that some generic activities, such as focusing on the client's knowledge of self, personal assets, limitations, aspirations, etc., are needed for effective counselling to take place. Generally speaking, it is the counsellor's responsibility to help each client understand and realize his or her potential for living a full and productive life. This implies that the counsellor will help clients arrive at and pursue any behavioral/attitudinal changes that are necessary to have positive personal development in their lives.

There are other factors which impinge on the role of counsellors in today's changing society. There is the need for counsellor today to see themselves working as "part of a team" and not trying to go it alone in professional isolation. Post modern society is a global, complex network of interacting systems and sub-systems. It offers endless challenges and opportunities to its individual members. The success of our social structure ultimately depends on the contribution of each member. Counselling psychologists, being socially conscious and thus aware of this, should assume responsibility for their contribution to it. No longer is it possible, professionally, to work as atomistic isolates. Counselling psychologists must accept the fact that they have to interact, at least in a consultative capacity, not only with each other but with other professionals. This includes those who may or may not be directly involved in the helping professions. This consultation is especially crucial with those who are specifically involved in the lives of their clients. Often it is within the context of these consultative sessions that counselling psychologists can become aware of ways to help their clients and learn to accept their own limitations as well as confirm their assets. It is important to remember that the main concern of the counsellor is the welfare of the individual operating within the context of the social structure. Most individuals who seek help from the counsellor are surrounded by others who share this concern. A counsellor can benefit by establishing and maintaining open contact with these significant others. This "systems" approach can be very meaningful for counsellors in that it enriches their resource base and enhances their knowledge of their clients. It is the counsellor's responsibility, unless otherwise directed by the client, to involve significant others in the counselling process. In fact, I believe that this interactive process by counsellors should extend beyond significant others and involve other existing services such as Public Health, Mental Health Associations, etc., in the community.

Counselling Modes

In North American culture, the practice of counselling psychology has followed two modes of operation. These modes are individual counselling, that is, the counselling of one client by one counsellor, and group counselling, the use of group interaction to facilitate self-understanding and individual behavior change. Although individual and group counselling may have undergone some changes in their procedures and composition, they have remained consistent for many years and are still used as a main basis for working with clients.

Of these two modes, individual counselling is the more traditional and well known counselling procedure. It originated in modern times from such practices as the Freudian process of analysis and has dominated the practice of those engaged in the helping professions for much of the past 50 years. Individual counselling has no boundaries in its application and can be an effective method of counselling in almost any situation. Mahler (1969) suggests that individual counselling would be beneficial, although not necessarily essential, in some or all of the following situations:

1. When the client is in a state of crisis.

2. When the client's need for attention is too great to be managed in a group.
3. When the client has a very limited awareness of his or her own feelings, motivations and behaviors.
4. When the client is grossly ineffective in the area of interpersonal relationship skills.
5. When confidentiality is essential to protect the client.

There is a view that too much emphasis has been placed on individual counselling. This view has been given credence with the development of such practices and theories of counselling as systems theory, family counselling, as well as group counselling (Davidson, 1983; Gazda, 1971; Satir, 1972). The proponents of these practices believe that much of what is done in individual work can actually be done as effectively and efficiently in groups of peers and/or by working with and through the client's significant others.

While recognizing the systemic and/or consultative approaches as effective methods of counselling, there are, as Mahler (1969) points out, situations where individual counselling is regarded as the preferred option. In my opinion, such situations exist in current practice and the use of individual counselling continues to be appropriate today.

In situations where counsellors feel that individual counselling is necessary, they initially have a responsibility to create a relationship with their clients that includes a positive environment, a genuine concern, unconditional acceptance and empathetic understanding. However, having established such a relationship, counsellors should try to extend the relationship to include others outside the confines of the counselling setting. In doing so the counsellor can become aware of the total life experiences of the client, which is a necessary step in seeing the client in context. To accomplish this it is necessary to meet personally with some of the client's significant others in situations outside "the office." There are several ways that the counsellor can achieve this without breaching confidentiality. In private practice clinics, for example, the counsellor could try to become more aware of the client's life outside the counselling setting. In school situations, the counsellor could endeavor to casually meet with students in the corridors where groups gather, or spend some time visiting classrooms and consulting with teachers. Interactions with significant others in these ways will enable the counsellor to broaden understanding and thus gain valuable insight into the socio-political and interpersonal life of the client. This kind of ecosystemic involvement will enhance the counsellor's understanding of the client and thereby add new insight into the helping process.

The second mode of counselling most used in practice today is group counselling. Developed since the 1960s, group counselling is a dynamic, interpersonal process focusing on conscious thought and behavior. It is characterized by therapy functions such as permissiveness, orientation to reality, catharsis, mutual trust, caring, understanding, acceptance and support. These therapy functions are created and nurtured through the sharing of personal struggles in a small group (usually 5-12) persons consisting of one's peers and the counsellor. The group consists of individuals with various concerns which are not necessarily debilitating to the extent of requiring extensive personality change (Gazda, 1971, 1977; Corey & Corey, 1988; George and Dustin, 1988). Through the process of group counselling, the participants hope to increase an understanding of their difficulties and arrive at solutions to their problems. With the support of others who have had similar problems, the participants hope that positive change will follow (George & Christiani, 1990).

Group counselling is sought after by many different kinds of groups such as real men, feminist groups, recovering alcoholics groups, abusive spouses groups, etc. Group counselling can be used to deal with a wide range of problems, for example, sexual dysfunction, marital difficulties, self-awareness, career decision making, personal growth, etc. In group counselling the participants form a support for people who are often trapped in a mode of self-destructive behavior which needs the support of others who have suffered similar trauma in the past or are experiencing similar problems in the present. The dynamics of group counselling provide a nurturing environment of trust and acceptance where clients support one another and journey through their personal struggles together. In group counselling the participants feel the need to discuss these problems within the context of group interaction.

The goal of group counselling can be to prevent problems from arising and/or to keep already existing problems from becoming larger and perhaps interfering with the participants' intra- as well as their interpersonal development.

The role of the counselling psychologist in group counselling is similar in many ways to that of the counsellor engaged in individual counselling. As in individual counselling, the counsellor in group counselling must establish a relationship built on trust and acceptance. Concomitant with these basic counselling skills, the counsellor who works with groups must have the additional skills necessary to "facilitate" the group without "controlling," and to "confront" without "disempowering." This requires a deep understanding of one's own personal belief system regarding democracy and power as well as a comprehensive understanding of group dynamics. This understanding demands the skill of being able to follow unobtrusively and intervene effectively in patterns of communication both verbal and non-verbal that develop within the group between the clients themselves as well as between the client and the counsellor. This process is not unlike that followed by family therapists such as Satir (1964). An understanding and appreciation of body language (non-verbal communication) is crucial in understanding and managing group processes.

There is one very different element operating in group counselling that does not exist in individual counselling, namely, the group's composition. Often this will be the complicating mix which can influence the practice and procedures the counsellor will follow. A counsellor usually has little control in choosing the various personality types that comprise a group. The personalities in any group may be similar or they may differ entirely. However, all groups will eventually develop their own identity.

Sharing the Role

Within the context of these two pivotal modes of group and individual counselling, the counsellor has many mini roles that are played out in everyday work. Many of these related roles have been jealously guarded and enshrined in the belief and hence the practice of "traditional minded" counselling psychologists that the counsellor is the only person who can work with the client at any given time. This belief leads to the practice of the counsellor taking sole and full responsibility for helping to bring about change in the beha-vior/attitude of the individual client. This approach is a dated and an outmoded practice for counselling in the 21st century.

This belief by counsellors that they are the sole helper in solving the clients problems arises from today's job expectations of counsellors. In post modern society, counselling psychologists, not unlike people in other helping professions, have had to spend most of their professional time dealing with crisis or at best, remedial counselling. Because of the unpredictability of situations in which individuals find themselves, crisis counselling today is a necessary and integral part of the work of the counsellor. This emphasis on crisis situations has left an important aspect of counselling in the background, namely, preventive or developmental counselling. Preventive counselling, although it does not have the dramatic effects that one sees in crisis counselling, can have long term positive effects and can prevent problems from occurring in the future.

Preventive counselling is built on the belief that if a person becomes involved in certain kinds of negative behaviors, even though they may not be perceived as too serious at the moment, such behaviors can become more serious or negative in the future. Ideally it ought to be a major part of the role of the counsellor to attempt to identify these behaviors and thus intervene in order to avoid more serious problems in the future. It seems obvious that an emphasis on preventive counselling would be a sensible road for counselling psychologists to follow. However, because of financial cutbacks and clients' demands for here and now solutions to their problems, more and more emphasis is placed on crisis/remedial, brief counselling. As a result of this, the counsellor is seen as the person who is on site "to fix" a crisis situation. In other words, counselling has become basically reactive or at best, remedial. As a result, counsellors spend a lot of their time working individually with seriously troubled clients. Consequently, because of these pressures, it has become necessary for counsellors to forego a more active role in prevention.

To compensate for the demand for crisis counselling, and thus, lack of time spent in a preventive role, counsellors have to seriously consider sharing their role with other "helpers" in the institution and community. Counsellors have to face up to the reality that they can no longer afford the luxury of the neat Freudian nomenclature of "individual therapist/healer." They have to incorporate into their role a more pedagogical position in order to cope with present day needs and live within the realities of the demands of post modern society which asks for more for less. If counsellors fail to recognize this need for role sharing, many clients living in the present stringent socio-economic reality will suffer the more negative effects of not being able to find help at the preventative stage of their problems. In the realities of the post modern world, counsellors have to assume a more open (holistic) approach to their professional practice in regards to working with individual clients. They must be able and willing to attack the problems of society not only as counsellor/therapists but also as teachers and leaders. Thus the need arises for a more collaborative/sharing approach within the counselling practice among significant others in the client's life and among other professionals in the life of the counsellor.

The need for a more collaborative/pedagogical approach, apart from its value as a counselling tool, has been exacerbated by the growing acceptance of the philosophy of rational economics and its consequent financial cutbacks, particularly in the human services sectors within society. Not unlike workers in other helping professions, counselling psychologists have to accept the reality that they can no longer act alone and expect to "solve" all the immediate problems of their clients. They have to accept the inevitable, namely, that they must look beyond themselves as the sole healer/therapist and use the many other human resources that are available to them and their clients. They must realize that they can effectively help their clients by using in the counselling process the expertise of other available personnel. Using other personnel requires counselling psychologists to extend their practice to include other social systems that surround and impact on their clients. Counselling should be carried out on a continuum. No one person can give all the help necessary, that is, be all things to all persons. Each and every educator in the school, every health worker in a hospital, or for that matter, every counsellor in private practice should consider themselves to be members of a team, sharing their counselling techniques and duties with co-professionals and para-professionals (Lusterman, 1988; Hollis & Hollis, 1965). This team approach gives the counselling process a greater depth and breadth. Counsellors in the context of today's social milieu cannot function effectively in isolation. The counselling psychologist in the 21st century needs to create a practice based on a cooperative, team approach.

Establishing a collaborative/consulting team consisting of significant others is of inestimable value in order to bring about effective counselling. It emphasizes the need for counsellors to establish communication and foster involvement with the "systems" surrounding their clients. This more open approach to counselling comes under many labels, including systemic, consultative and ecological counselling and collaborative work and is discussed in Chapter 5.

Needs Identification

Counselling implies that there is a need within the individual community and/or institution which requests its service. It is therefore part of the counsellor's role to identify this need(s). In a general sense, needs refer to the physiological and/or psychological requirements that a person must meet to properly function as a self-fulfilled and productive individual within society (Maslow, 1968). If counsellors are to help fulfil the needs of their clients, they must, through consultation, become aware of what these needs are. Once counsellors are aware of their clients' needs, they must prioritize them in terms of their urgency (Dixon & Glover, 1985). This is necessary from the point of view of being in touch with the reasons counselling is requested. Prioritizing needs can also be of inestimable value to counsellors because it helps prevent unproductive and sometimes even unnecessary commitments, thus leading to a more effective use of their counselling time (Dryden & Feltham, 1992). For instance, if the need for family consultation is seen as greater than that of individual counselling, then it is obviously better to put one's energies into that area.

Assessing Individual Needs and Setting Goals

Having assessed the general needs of the institution or community, the counsellor has to now assess the needs of the individuals within the institution. The needs of clients who seek counselling are many and varied. Persons who are referred or who seek counselling may have personal, social and/or career development needs. This wide range of needs can be broken down into interpersonal needs, which includes relationships with peers, significant others, family, etc.; intrapersonal needs, such as emotional instability, self-understanding, self-esteem, etc.; and career development needs. The identification of the specific needs of clients is a difficult and complex process. Clients who come for counselling often have only a superficial understanding of their needs. Usually they come somewhat confused about why they are there and what to expect from counselling. Counselling psychologists, because of this confusion on the part of the clients, need to help them clarify what their problems and concerns are, in other words, why they are there in the counsellor's office. It is therefore incumbent on the counsellor to help them define their needs and help them set goals towards fulfilling them. In a clinical situation this identification is generally done through the initial interview(s). If the counsellor is employed by an institution, such as a school or a hospital, there are additional avenues s/he can follow to supplement and enhance this process. Some of these are active consultation with significant others in the institution, and/or an analyses of any anecdotal records, etc. that might be available within the institution (Dainow & Bailey, 1988; Eagan, 1994; Kolb, 1984; Culley, 1991). A more specific way that needs can be assessed, particularly if the counsellor is working within an institution, is through an assessment procedure.

Assessment can be divided into two basic categories, formal assessment and informal assessment. Informal assessment refers to the use of methods, such as observation and interviews, which do not necessarily use standard psychological tests. Formal assessment, on the other hand purports to objectively measure an individual's behavior in a standard situation. This would include methods such as the use of IQ tests and/or personality profiles (Robertson, 1988).

The literature generally refers to four basic functions of assessment (George & Cristiani, 1990; Hansen, Stevic, and Warner, 1982):

1. Prediction: helping to predict a client's degree of success in a course of study, job or career.
2. Diagnosis: assisting both the counsellor and the client gain insight into strengths and weaknesses of the client.
3. Monitoring: helping to monitor the progress that a client is making.
4. Evaluation: helping to assess the client's growth, the counsellor's success or achievement of specific goals. Some of the more common areas of assessment are:
   a. Intelligence – group
   b. Intelligence – individual
   c. Aptitude
   e. Achievement
   f. Interest inventories
   g. Personality profiles
   h. Behavior rating scales

Following the assessment process and the identification of needs, the counsellor must then establish a course of action to meet those needs. Following are four procedures used by counsellors in setting up this course of action. Most counsellors will use all of these to a lesser or greater extent depending on their particular counselling orientation (Dainow and Bailey, 1988).

1. Set the Goals for the Counselling Process

These goals can be general, long term or indeed they can be just some specific objectives. Kolb (1984) sets forth a paradigm or model for goal setting which emphasizes the experiential life of the client. Clients will learn new or will change old behaviors when the goals established are within, or at least somehow related, to their personal theory or life experiences (Dainow & Bailey, 1988; Kanfir & Goldstein, 1986; Rogers, 1951).

2. Plan Strategies to Reach the Goals

Learning through counselling, like learning through teaching, requires a process of active participation and not simply passive reaction or worse, inaction, on the part of the learner. Strategies, like goals, should be related to or connect somehow with the personal life of the client. They should, to some extent, reflect the client's personal constructs which gave meaning to their experienced reality (Kelly, 1955).

3. Carry out or Implement the Planned Strategy

This procedure is not actually separate from planning. However, counsellors should be cognizant that it may be necessary, but not necessarily sufficient, to talk about or discuss strategy. Strategic planning should be reflective and should generate new ideas and new thinking about the counselling process for the counsellor as well as for the client. The success of this process of reflection and analysis into what could (should) happen and how to bring it about will be highly related to the actual outcome. At this stage in the counselling process both the counsellor and the client should consider some form of contractual (written or verbal) arrangement to commit both the counsellor and the client to the planned strategy. This action based planning reflects the Dewey (1938) learning theory that we learn best by doing.

4. Evaluation

The final stage in the plan of action is to evaluate how efficiently the previous three steps have been working. Counselling is about enabling people to change, to gain more control over and to assume more responsibility for their lives. To accomplish these goals, counsellors should always question if what they are doing in the counselling process is accomplishing the task. They should also be very aware of the importance of the client's input and involvement in the evaluation stage of the counselling process. This input and involvement by the client is crucial because it is during this evaluative stage of counselling that the issues related to power and control in counselling come to the forefront.

Power Sharing in the Counselling Process

Ideally in the counselling relationship, power is shared by both the client and the counsellor. However, there often exists a power imbalance, which for the most part weighs heaviest on the side of the counsellor. In the initial interview, the counsellor usually takes the lead and assumes control of the process. This is necessary because of the clients' often confused state in the beginning stages of counselling. Ideally, when the initial discovery period is completed, the counsellor should begin to share and gradually return control of the process to the client. Sometimes counsellors find it difficult to do this. They hold on to control of the process, which clients, because of their initial feelings of inadequacy and vulnerability, gave them in the beginning. The difficulty experienced by counsellors in sharing control with their clients raises questions regarding the exercise of power in the counselling relationship.

The counselling process, by its very nature, involves power. The mere fact that persons come to another for help implies they are making an assumption that here is someone who can help, or give assistance, and thus s/he is in some kind of power position. Counsellors should be aware of this assumption on the part of clients and, from an ethical point of view at least, minimize the client's sense of powerlessness. How counsellors deal with this issue of power depends to a large extent on what the individual counsellor's belief system is regarding the process of counselling and how counsellors perceive their relationship with the client. If counsellors believe that they have "the answers" to clients' problems, then it is very likely that counsellors will use their position of power to impose their decisions on the client. In this situation clients are often led to believe that, regardless of how they may feel, the best way to proceed is in the direction that the counsellor has established. In other words, the client is led to believe that because the counsellor offers one solution, there is no need to consider alternatives. On the other hand, if the counsellor accepts the client/counsellor relationship as one of enabling and not solely of directing, then the counsellor will assume an "empowering" as opposed to an "overpowering" position and allow the client to be an equal participant in the four steps of counselling.

Power sharing in counselling is in sync with post modern views of interpersonal relationships. These views stress the importance of giving voice to those who previously were not heard (Giroux, 1988). Power, epitomized by the inability to listen to and accept with understanding the voice of the client, will lead to failure in planned strategies and hence failure in counselling goals. The voices of clients are often the very embodiment of their vision of what is best for them. Their voices are their experiences and give purpose to their life. It is the professional duty of the counsellor to help clients realize and give practical application to their voices. In doing so, counsellors will develop a shared vision and goal with the client and will commit to working together to attain them.

Power is an issue that permeates the totality of counselling. However, it has particular relevance and significance during the process of evaluation. Evaluation in counselling is more than simply reassessing the counselling process concerning what the counsellor and the client are doing. It is more than challenging the goals and strategies previously agreed to. Evaluation in counselling is a process whereby the client and counsellor share visions and give their voice to what they believe should or could happen. A major part of the evaluative process should be concerned with ensuring that the client is "enabled" to share in the decision making and thus be an equal player in the counselling process. In a sense, evaluation procedures in counselling should be used to redefine and re-establish ownership of the process and help to define power relationships within it (Dainow & Bailey, 1988). In counsellor/client relationships, as in physician/patient relationship, the counsellor has the power to influence and sometimes to "greatly" influence the thoughts, feelings and thus the present and future behavior of the client. To obtain optimal success for the client in counselling, counsellors ought to be always conscious of this reality and use their power professionally.

Counsellor's Role In Client Career/Job Placement

Due to the socio-political/economic conditions in today's society, there is a growing demand for counselling in the areas of career choice and work access. Consequently, in many institutions and, indeed, in private practices, educational and/or work placement has become a part of the counsellor's role. Counselling in these areas involves some or all of the following: helping clients to take concrete action in furthering their education, assisting clients in finding a first job, helping clients move from unemployment to employment, or from underemployment to more suitable employment. Through counselling interviews, information groups and/or career education classes, clients explore career opportunities, procedures for locating a job, completing applications, interview techniques and so forth. Since placement in a job is the desired conclusion of the process of career-exploration, which includes self-exploration and decision making (Srebalus, Marinelli & Messing, 1982), it is important that counsellors, who practice within this area of counselling, establish and maintain a good relationship with business agencies and employment centres.

Career/job placement counselling places new demands on the role of counselling psychologists in the 21st century. Counsellors working specifically in this area of counselling are expected to be able to recommend certain levels of educational and/or work placement for clients. Because of the instability within the work world, hence the ever-changing and uncertain future of jobs, this is often quite a complex task. It requires counsellors and clients to know and use all available information regarding the nature and future of the educational institution or work place to enable them to place clients where they can benefit most. Counsellors must have a full understanding of what various institutions offer and expect of their students. Clients must be helped to understand how educational choices relate to life's goals both educationally and occupationally. The counsellor's role is to work with clients to find the best choices (of education and/or work place) to suit their needs and abilities (Hansen, Stevic and Warner, 1986).

The area of educational placement also involves the development of orientation programs. Orientation includes all activities which individuals can use to develop a realistic relationship with their total environment. Orientation services are needed by clients throughout their lives, but they are particularly important during crucial points of change and decision-making in their initial stages of career development. In institutions such as grade schools, orientation programs are generally designed to help students/clients make a smooth transition from one school level to another or from school to work.

The role of the career counsellor should also include follow-up studies of clients. Research of this kind can be very valuable for the counsellor as well as the institution. In carrying out follow-up studies, the counsellor collects and analyzes data on clients who have had career/job placement counselling in the past. Data collected through follow-up studies enables counsellors to reflect on the effectiveness of their career counselling procedures. It also helps meet the criteria for accountability demanded in all professions today. Follow-up studies can also become an integral part of the research component of counselling and can provide both the counsellor and the institution with valuable insight in relation to the relevancy of their role and philosophy in providing good and appropriate career programs (Cramer et al., 1970). Career counselling is discussed in more detail in Chapters 6 & 7.

Other Influences that Impact on the Role of the Counsellor

Discussion regarding the role of the counsellor must not fail to include the influences on that role by their place of work. Today, despite an increase in the number of counselling psychologists in private practice, many counsellors are employed by institutions or agencies. It is both professionally and personally significant that the hiring agency or institution have a commitment to, as well as an expectation of, the work of the counsellor. This expectation and commitment should be based on a broad understanding of counselling content and process. The socio-political and economic climate of today emphasizes the need for smaller, yet more efficient services. It also regards the needs of the group as taking precedence over the needs of the individual. In this climate, counselling tends to be seen as one of the areas where so-called "downsizing" can easily be done. Although in most institutions there is a general agreement about the need for counselling, there is often confusion about how best to make use of its potential.

In general, it can be said that the institution which commits itself to provide counselling services for its workers or members should have an understanding of, and a commitment to, the practice. This commitment should include an understanding of the work of the counsellor and the promotion of this understanding among all employees. This recognition and understanding by employers will enhance the understanding of the true value of counselling among employees. It will also encourage other employees to become involved in the practice and encourage those who need counselling to be more accepting of it.

Employers should also be aware that counsellors, like other professionals, need to have time and opportunity to network with co-professionals and professionals in related areas of work. Today, because of work overload, lack of funding for professional development, and because in many institutions there is only one counsellor on staff, counsellors often find themselves professionally isolated. Institutions should be aware of this fact and its detrimental effects on the work and the personal life of the counsellor. Because of this isolation, organizations should do all they can to facilitate a system of networking among counsellors and other workers in the helping professions. This could be done through the provision of computer technology and Internet networking. However, electronic interaction is not enough. Feelings of isolation are brought on by lack of interpersonal contact, hence the need for some person to person interaction. This can be accommodated through conferences and/or other forums of people interaction. This will not only help counsellors in their own professional growth, but will have a positive effect on their commitment to the institution and to their clients.

Counsellors, like employers, also have a duty to be committed to the profession. This commitment is germane to the very notion of counselling. Counselling, unlike other professions, has its rewards not so much in the outcomes, which are often obscure and/or even unnoticed, but in the quality of time and commitment that is put into the process. This commitment involves a dedication to professionalism as well as to the goals of the individual, the institution and society as a whole. For example, counsellors who work in an educational setting should have a commitment to contribute to the goals of the institution as they relate to the social, emotional and educational well being of the individual within that institution. In a society which tends to de-emphasize the individual and emphasize greater concern for the group, the present day counsellor needs to be a committed and firm voice that will ensure that the rights and freedoms of the individual are not eroded by a collective, so-called neo-conservative philosophy. In so doing, counsellors achieve the most satisfaction for themselves, their clients and the institution in which they work.

The role of the post modern counsellor must also be open to include the option of a systems approach to counselling. This commitment to work more closely with significant others in the life of the client, such as parents or guardians, teachers, social workers and physicians, etc., is not without its benefits. This would necessarily commit the counsellor to establishing a professional network among systems within the community where s/he works and should contribute to the overall goals of the client as well as the institution.

Also impinging on the role of the counsellor are the client's expectations of the counsellor. Many clients come to counselling with inflated or unrealistic expectations. They do not have a clear understanding of their problems and they expect the counsellor to provide immediate solutions for these problems. The counselling process works much more efficiently when the client understands its possibilities and limitations. Therefore, it is incumbent on counsellors to define their role early in the counselling process and to inform the client that counselling is a slow process that ultimately requires the client to be the one who acts, decides, changes and becomes (George and Cristiani, 1990). By encouraging clients to discuss their expectations of the counselling experience, both counsellors and clients can avoid later disappointments and misunderstandings.

Besides this insight into the counselling process, it is only reasonable for the client to expect that the counsellor will bring to the counselling session a broad knowledge and understanding of human behavior and a keen insight into why people act the way they do. Coupled with this is the expectation that the counsellor know WHAT to do, and more to the point, what possibilities are open to clients, which will help them become more capable of coping with their particular difficulty. This implies that the counsellor must be able to assist clients in the exploration of their emotions and in decision making, both for short and long term plans.

The Counselling Psychologist as Consultant

Adhering strictly to an individual approach to counselling psychology is often criticized as "dealing primarily with the casualties of our society rather than attempting to change those institutions, organizations, systems, and communities that contribute to individual problems" (Thorne & Dryden, 1993; George & Cristiani, 1990). For this and other reasons counsellors are redefining their role to include less individual counselling and more consultation.

Consultation can be defined as a collaborative relationship through which the counsellor, working with significant others such as parents, social workers, physicians, families, etc., can communicate their concerns about and seek solutions to the client's problems. In a consultative role, the counsellor serves as an educator, facilitator and collaborator to individuals or groups (Stein, 1990). According to Kutzik (1979), consultation is a time limited relationship of professional peers in which the consultee voluntarily seeks the advice of the consultant regarding a specific case or problem and decides whether or not to take this advice (p. 5). As consultants, counsellors can use their training in group work, human relations, decision-making and conflict resolution to bring about a better understanding of the ways in which significant others can (may) assist in helping the client. Counsellors can thus enable significant others to provide help which they might otherwise feel to be beyond their abilities or their particular sphere of influence.

This view of counsellor as consultant makes professional sense. Consultation enhances the counsellor's knowledge and understanding of clients and their problems. It can also give the counsellor "more personal time" in a society where almost all counsellors are working with a limited amount of time and money. For instance, counsellors who work in schools have historically perceived themselves as the sole source of help for individual students within the school. Counsellors have traditionally seen themselves as being ineffective if they did not have direct contact, either individually or in small groups, with all students seeking counselling. Because of the large student-counsellor ratio in most schools, this awesome task actually limited counsellor-student contact. Frequently, those few students experiencing the most obvious problems monopolized a majority of the counsellor's time. As a result, many students received few counselling services and indeed, some students who experienced less obvious problems, were overlooked. More recently, counselling psychologists are becoming aware of the influence of the family and community on a client's life and recognize the benefits of involving both in the counselling process. As a result, counsellors are refocusing many of their counselling efforts to include and consult with both other professionals and significant others within the community in which the client lives. Counsellors are consulting and working with families, and serving as "linking agents" between community resources and client's needs and problems. In expanding their role to include consultation, counsellors broaden the basis of support both for their work and for their clients' well being. For example, by consulting with parents, counsellors can help them gain a better and broader understanding of the various developmental stages that the child has to go through to reach maturity. This knowledge can be of help to the parent in trying to understand and cope with the various behavioral changes that the child exhibits throughout his/her emotional/physical development. This knowledge can help prevent "normal" developmental problems from being perceived by the parent or guardian as some form of abnormality or neurosis. The consultative process in counselling can therefore be used very effectively in preventive or developmental counselling. Consultation has an additional benefit, in that it creates the perception that the counselling process is educational rather than therapeutic. This perception causes less resistance in people to become involved in counselling.

Consulting, not unlike other human interactions, has its problems. However, as Singh (1994) suggests, having clear purposes, goals and realistic expectations of the process minimizes these difficulties (p. 40).

Limitations in Counselling Psychology

The post modern context calls for a counselling practice that is more systems oriented and skill sharing in its practice. This position is based on the belief that there are no experts in any particular specialty or indeed, there are no specialty areas. It posits that the role of the counsellor is that of "non-expert" and one of "helper" among equals. However, there also coexists with the post modern thought the modernist belief in specialized training. This position holds that certain problems need some form of "specialized" counselling that only "specially" trained counsellors possess. This position suggests that counsellor educators should give some serious thought to the notion of "counsellor specialization" in counsellor education programs. The modernist belief holds that training in specific "specialty types" of counselling ought to be available, for example, counselling abused children, counselling the aged, adolescent counselling, career development counselling, family counselling, divorce counselling, gay and lesbian counselling, etc.

In the global post modern world, which is fraught with social, economic and spiritual uncertainty, the demand for counselling is growing rapidly. Counsellors are being presented with a great variety of problems with a wide range of difficulty. In light of this it is important for counsellors to be aware of the particular belief systems regarding specialists, generalists and non-expert helpers. There are strengths and weaknesses in all of these positions. Counsellors must recognize these various philosophies, weigh their merits and practice their profession within the particular philosophy of their choice.

Counselling psychology purports to help a wide and diverse group of clients, who present a wide range of problems including social, emotional, educational, career, and intra- and interpersonal. Some problems presented by clients may require collaborative work with others in the helping professions, such as psychiatrists, public health workers, physicians or social workers, while others may need help from clients' co-workers or family members and others can be solved through single interaction between client and counsellor. Counselling includes working not only with individual clients, but also their significant others, such as parents, spouses, supervisors, etc. Confronted with this plethora of difficulties and problems, counsellors should, regardless of whether they adhere to the modernist or post modernist belief systems regarding the delivery of their services, ought to be aware of which range of problems they feel comfortable with and which they feel they can help clients resolve. Limitations in counselling are not necessarily only skill or technique driven but to a large degree are philosophy driven. The limits then are based not solely in the "specialization demands of the trade" but in the practitioner's belief systems that underpin the practice.

This chapter gives a brief overview of some aspects of the role of the counselling psychologist. It has stressed the need for counsellors to look at their role, with its limitations, in the light of post modern society. We are living in a new and changing social milieu. Counselling psychologists must take the time to rethink their roles from the perspective of these changing times. There are many and varied factors that relate to and impinge upon the general practice of counselling psychology in post modern society. The counselling psychology profession is inextricably intertwined with the total social fabric and as it continues to grow and mature it must accept its role as non-static and evolutionary. Counselling has grown, and continues to grow, out of a need for self-development and social connectedness in a society that has radically changed from a secure and stable value-defined system to one that is value confusing and ever-changing. The role of the counsellor in this changing social milieu has to be inclusive and based on a practice that incorporates a holistic, systemic and consultative philosophy.

Chapter 4
Personal Qualities of the Counselling Psychologist

People who aspire to the profession of counselling psychology are not unlike persons who aspire to other professions. They are unique individuals with their own sets of personal values and beliefs. However, persons who aspire to the profession of counselling must possess certain additional characteristics or attributes to be true counsellors. The counselling process is necessarily influenced not only by values, personal belief systems and cultural biases, but also by the personal practical theory of the counsellor. The presence of these values and belief systems can have a major impact on the outcome of counselling with different clients in different situations. In fact, they can often determine whether the counselling process and outcome is effective or ineffective (Rogers, 1951; Culley, 1991; Vriend, 1985; Tyler, 1969). The combination of personal characteristics, sound professional knowledge and specific counselling skills constitutes an effective counselling professional. The following is a discussion of some of the necessary, but not necessarily sufficient, personal and professional qualities which persons in the counselling profession ought to have, or at least strive to possess.

Personal Characteristics

Personal attributes (personality traits) are individually specific and in many cases, immutable. Attributes such as empathy, sincerity, congruence and personal regard, etc., which are germane to the very essence of counselling, are as difficult to create as they are to change. Counsellors cannot simply "put on" desirable counselling attributes like a costume before a performance and remove it directly afterwards. Counsellors must at least have the predisposition for those characteristics, which are necessary to facilitate and enable the counselling process. The expectation is that all counsellors will have these basic qualities. In any event, it is the responsibility of both counsellor educators and counsellors to develop and foster within their personal lives, through practice and reflection, these core counselling personal qualities. In addition, there are other, no less desirable personal/professional qualities which counsellors should aim towards or strive for. The following will highlight some of these more obvious qualities.

A Caring Relationship

Counsellors, like others who work in the helping professions, should be able to establish reasonable and caring interpersonal relationships with their clients and other professionals. These relationships should be based on mutual trust and ought to be genuine, empathetic and sincere. Such positive caring relationships can only be established with clients when counsellors believe that it is within the nature of people to enhance and enrich their own personal development and fulfillment through open and honest relationships (Culley, 1991; George and Cristiani, 1990; Rogers, 1951). When such a relationship is established, counsellors can genuinely give a message to clients that they (the counsellor) do believe in their (the clients') inner strengths and that they truly care for their clients' well being.

The attribute of positive caring is an essential characteristic for good interpersonal relationships. It is also a positive and necessary condition for effective counselling, which underlies most, if not all, of the other general counselling attributes. However, caring can be a double edged sword, as it can also be used by the counsellor to achieve negative outcomes. These negative outcomes can result from the way the counsellor presents caring to his/her clients. Caring has to be given to the client in an objective and non-possessive way and should offer the client a frank, open and non-possessive relationship. This relationship should not suggest indebtedness to the counsellor on the part of the client nor should it imply ownership of the client by the counsellor. Genuine caring implies honesty, openness and a belief in the rights of the client to be free to personally develop independently from, rather than tied to, the influence of the counsellor. In other words, counsellors should show that they care by empowering each client to grow and develop as the client sees fit. Counsellors should not use the skill of caring as a source of power to make clients fit the kind of mold the counsellor wants and thinks is best for them.

The concept of power and control of the individual by society and/or other individuals has been a popular topic in the writings of the post modern era. Foucault (1980), talks about the various techniques that are used by society in order to control or gain control over persons. Two of these techniques are normalization and totalization. Normalization is defined as the demand that those we teach or work with conform to a set standard which we hold as the norm, while totalization is putting all (everyone) into similar categories of behavior, for example, "all my clients do this or all my students act this way."

Such power techniques have important implications for counsellors practicing in the post modern society. They are subtle and give immense power to the person using them. It is easy for the "directive" minded counsellor to grab on to such techniques and use them as a way of exercising power over his/her clients. Such techniques, coupled with and used under the guise of caring, can be a dangerous mix in the hands of the counsellor who feels the need for power and control in the counselling process.

Institutions that offer counsellor education programs should ensure that such programs have components that offer students the opportunity to reflect on and analyze their personal development and personality traits. Aspiring counselling students need to become aware of their belief systems and personal theories regarding the true meaning of caring and to recognize its relationship to the use of power in counselling. If the institution feels that certain students possess personal characteristics which might adversely affect clients in the counselling relationship, then there should be a mechanism in place to confront these negative personality traits in students. Counselling should then be made available for such students to enable them to either modify these negative traits or change their particular career path. Failure to do this makes counsellor educators contributors to the practice of using the caring relationship as a opportunity to engage in so-called "voyeuristic surveillance" of clients. Every precaution should be taken by counsellor educators to keep the counselling profession free of people who develop counselling relationships by using smooth, insincere mind games to gain power and control over their clients. Such power plays are often presented to clients in the guise of honest and sincere caring. The use of power in this way is paradoxical since the counselling profession, by its very nature, is meant to foster power sharing and empowerment.

Humor

A sense of humor is an invaluable aid to all those who work on a regular basis with the troubled, challenged and/or the disadvantaged in our society. The value of humor in the counselling process has been long recognized by counsellors who practice in the field. Humor is one of the marks of Maslow's (1968) theory of self-actualization. Kuhlman (1984) believes that humor can be the embodiment of self-actualization and can help detach the client emotionally from a given problem. Leone (1986) suggests that laughter can be used by counsellors as a means of relieving tension and that humor can often act as a lever to give both the counsellor and the client a little respite from the tension of the moment. He suggests a number of ways that counsellors can introduce a sense of humor to their work to help lighten the burdens of the day-to-day counselling process. The following are some of his suggestions:

1. Learn to enjoy work and surround yourself with things that you enjoy. Such things could be a painting or a favorite chair or indeed some knick-knacks that one finds amusing.
2. If you are not happy, don't try to pretend you are happy. Do something about it. If you are not happy it is impossible to make someone else happy.

3. Expand your range of activities. Dare to be a nerd at times, use role playing, do things you may not like because you are not good at them by pretending to be someone who can do them well.
4. Find a favorite comic, listen to a humorous tape, see a comedy movie, learn a joke or two, use humorous anecdotes and examples.
5. Restructure your day, change your routine, learn what your clients think is funny (p. 141).

While humor can ease the build up of stress that can often cloud the counselling process, it can also be used to re-focus the counselling process. Humor can often help both the counsellor and the client to see the situation from a different perspective. Counsellors who work constantly in problem situations should, according to Goodman (1983), be able to see the comic side of life. Both the counsellor and the comic have to appreciate the humor which is created out of the often contrasting juxtaposition, and farcicalness in life. This is an invaluable tool which can be used to ward of discouragement and cynicism, both of which can be the downfall and professional ruin of a counsellor.

From the client's point of view, a counsellor's humor can sometimes help alleviate those "too heavy" situations and can foster a more open and personally comfortable counselling atmosphere. Morreall (1983) states that "when a person with a sense of humor laughs in the face of his own failure, he is showing that his perspective transcends the situation he is in, and that he does not have an egocentric, overly precious view of his own endeavors. It is because he feels good about himself at a fundamental level that this or that set back is not threatening to him" (p. 106).

Although humor is recognized as an important part of the repertoire of the counselling psychologist, caution must be taken by counsellors to distinguish between humor that is used to produce laughter or a lighter atmosphere, and sarcastic humor, which is often only funny at the expense of the client (Vriend, 1985). Zinger (1985) suggests six constructive functions of humor in counselling – humor as healer; humor as creativity; humor as reframer; humor as relationship builder; humor as fun; and humor as therapy. Zinger goes on to suggest that empathy, acceptance and genuineness are the core factors in enabling humor.

All humor is not the same. Ziv (1984) in a similar vein to Zinger (1985) discusses two kinds of humor, creative humor and appreciative humor. Creative humor is "the ability to perceive relationships between people, objects, or ideas in an incongruous way, as well as the ability to communicate this perception to others. This communication may be verbal and elicits in others smiles or laughter. Appreciative humor is the ability to understand and enjoy messages containing humor creativity, as well as situations that are incongruous but not menacing" (p. 111).

Goodman (1983) talks about true humor. He distinguishes between humor that laughs at people and humor that laughs with people. He sees humor as capable of being constructive and destructive. To illustrate his point, Goodman (1983) gives the following example:

> Both "laughing with" and "laughing at" go for the jocular vein. "Laughing with" is based on caring and empathy, builds confidence, involves people in fun. In "laughing with" a person makes a choice to be the butt of jokes. "Laughing with" is amusing and invites people to laugh, is supportive, brings people closer together, leads to positive repartee and pokes fun at universal human foibles. "Laughing at," on the other hand, is based on contempt and insensitivity, destroys confidence through put-downs, excludes people and makes them the butt of jokes, is abusive and offends some people, is sarcastic, divides people, leads to one-downmanship cycle, and reinforces stereotypes by singling out a particular group as the "butt" of the joke (p. 11).

Goodman's (1983) distinction between "laughing with" and "laughing at" is best summed up in his words "humor is laughter made from pain – not pain inflicted by laughter" (p. 12).

Zinger (1985) picks up this theme by pointing out the destructive functions of humor, viewing humor as aggression, humor as superiority, humor as defense mechanism and humor as social distance. Kerr (1967) elaborates this point when he writes "comedy is never the gaiety of things, it is the groan made gay. Laughter is not man's (persons) first impulse, he cries first. Comedy always comes second, late after the fact. Comedy is really the underside of things after the rock of our hearts has been lifted" (p. 199).

We can look at humor in counselling as a means of relieving stress and easing the build up of stress. We can also look at humor in counselling as a way of refocusing and allowing us to see the other side of tragedy. It is a second look from a different perspective. It permits counsellors to see a grave situation through a different lens, retake the picture and reprint it from a more open, broader and less threatening perspective.

Self-Actualizing Person

Counselling is a profession that necessarily demands that its practitioners be broadly educated in and truly understanding of the many and varied characteristics that constitute the human condition. Counselling psychologists therefore should be professionals who can look at society not only as a giant conglomerate, but also as an aggregate of unique individuals who are self-fulfilling and self-determining. Counsellors need to be able to perceive that individuals have the right to be self-accepting and a duty to be accepting of others. At the same time, counsellors ought to be able to acknowledge that these individuals, because they are self-determined and self- directed, are capable of making decisions and living with the consequences of these decisions (Culley, 1991). Counsellors, because they specialize in human behavior both from the point of view of its development in the here and now and its potential for growth, should also be able to appreciate people as personally dynamic and constantly changing.

In order to appreciate and understand these various attributes in others, counsellors themselves have to be dynamic individuals who are change oriented and constantly striving towards personal growth and development. To accomplish this attribute, counsellors must have or at least be striving towards an understanding of themselves as persons who are continually growing towards actualization. This understanding of self leads to the personal courage to accept others as they are while recognizing their potential for behavioral and social change. They should embrace this potential, challenge it and use it to move both themselves and their clients towards positive growth, even in the face of its sometimes uncertain odds.

This important attribute of acceptance of others within society is an integral part of the growth towards personal actualization. Rogers (1951) talks about unconditional acceptance of clients. This is the ideal towards which counsellors should strive. Counsellors, although they may be well versed in the theory of empathy and unconditional acceptance, often let personal biases or prejudices get in the way of their counselling. Counsellors who can accept all clients as persons of worth, even those who are "strange" to them, are well on the way to personal actualization.

Acceptance of all people is not always easy. Sometimes the reality of social class and/or physical differences get in the way. Counsellors, because they are human and because they usually belong to the so-called middle class, may find it difficult to relate to people who have different values than their own. Counsellors are sometimes upset by clients whom they perceive as having lower-class attitudes and patterns of behavior. They are prone to look on these pattern of behavior as somewhat objectionable and deviant, based simply on their own perception of what constitutes acceptable behavior. In a post modern world, where the paradox of global understanding and acceptance and ethnic nationalism appear to co-exist, it is imperative that those who work within the helping professions be persons of non-prejudicial integrity and global tolerance.

Counsellors in a school setting, for example, sometimes find it difficult to deal with the so-called "other" or "lower" class student. The rewards for working with people of different values are not often immediate. It is important for counsellors to realize that people with different values and belief systems are not "wrong" but only "different." It is also important for counsellors to be cognizant that this works in reverse as well. They must understand that people of different values from us may also have a difficult time accepting our differences.

Counsellors sometimes accept a counselling position feeling full of confidence and zeal, only to be confronted with a so-called "undesirable" client who does not fit their beliefs of what people should be like. This can sometimes set the counsellor's "self-assurance" in a spin. However, these experiences, if accepted positively and seen from the total human perspective should be part of the counsellors journey towards actualization and indeed a true test of their suitability for counselling.

These are some of the self-actualizing characteristics which counsellors strive for but which they may not necessarily fully attain. However, counsellors are not expected to be super person but persons who are continually building towards a better, more actualized self.

Professionalism

In addition to the personal characteristics of self-understanding, acceptance of others and humor, etc., that counsellors need in order to work effectively with their clients, effective counselling also depends on the counsellors professional attributes. A professional is one whose practice is based on theoretical and esoteric knowledge, the acquisition of which requires a long period of education. In other words, one who is well versed in and dedicated to a particular field of endeavor. It is generally understood and accepted that counsellors are professionals. This presumes that the practice of counselling is couched within a sound theoretical framework and based on research knowledge. It also implies that the counsellor has acquired a minimum level of education and specialized training in counselling theory and techniques. This level of education and specialization is usually attained through study at the graduate level from a recognized post secondary institution.

The client who comes for counselling believes that the counsellor is a professional and that s/he has sought and acquired specialized knowledge through formal and informal education. The client believes that the counsellor can draw upon and use this knowledge to enhance the resolution of a practical problem being experienced by the client. To effectively help clients resolve their problems, the counsellor should have acquired specialized knowledge which is not readily available to, but is of significant importance to the client. To enhance and nurture this acquired specialized knowledge and thus develop sound professionalism, a counsellor must keep abreast of recent research in the counselling psychology field. This is necessary not only as a source of intellectual and emotional growth for the counsellor, but also as a contribution to the profession. Remaining current with the literature also helps counsellors feel good about their work and boost their self-esteem and confidence. There is evidence in the literature to suggest that high job satisfaction and high self-esteem are related to the ability to deal effectively with high levels of confusion and frustration which often accompany their work (Wiggens & Weslander, 1986).

Attaining formal preservice education, and allocating time in their working life for reading and research are essential ingredients for professionalism in counselling. However, in order for counsellors to continue to grow professionally, there also ought to be time to participate in other professional activities, such as collaboration with other professionals in the field and participation in professional conferences locally, nationally and internationally. Today, in a rapidly changing and global social climate highlighted by instant access to world information and communication, the phrase "no man (person) is an island" takes on a whole new literal meaning and ought to become the professional counsellor's motto. Professional activities will not only enhance the professionalism of the counsellor but, by interacting with other professionals who deal with similar problem clients, counsellors will be better able to understand and accept the presenting problems of their own clients and therefore become more professional and effective counsellors.

Chapter 5
Counselling: A Systems Approach

Emphasis has been placed throughout this book on the counsellor's role as one of sharing workload and collaboration. The counselling process is described as establishing a therapeutic relationship not only with the client, but also with significant others in the life of the client. Systems counselling encompasses within it all of the aspects of sharing and collaboration and regards counselling as an integrative and inclusive process which emphasizes the wholeness of the person, functioning as one with self and community.

Systems Theory

Science can be described as the discovery of knowledge. It is that branch of learning that helps us understand better our human and material universe. It differs from technology in so far as technology is concerned with the implementation or application of scientific knowledge.

Science, through the intervention of homo sapiens, has for most of its history been categorized into separate specializations such as engineering, biology, chemistry, physics, psychology, mathematics, etc. These "specialties" continue to operate independently of each other and have been thought of and treated by professionals who work within them as separate, unique and independent disciplines. This separation of science into discrete disciplines was a viable practice in the very early days of scientific discoveries and technological implementation, when for example, as Bertalanffy (1968) points out, our scientific knowledge was limited to electronic and/or mechanical discoveries such as the steam engine and the wireless. Considered scientific breakthroughs in their time, these discoveries were sustainable and capable of functioning in isolation within their specific area or specialty. However, with the evolution of more complex knowledge, and the development of highly complicated and complex electromechanical machines, for example, computers and space vehicles, this simple isolated approach to scientific achievements is no longer viable or indeed possible (Bertalanffy, 1968).

The advanced scientific discoveries of today and their consequent technologies are only possible when they are seen as conglomerates of the various "independent" disciplines such as engineering, mechanics, electronics, psychology, chemistry, biology, sociology, etc. These and other so called "independent" sciences are now seen as "interdependent" and function efficiently and effectively only through cooperative interaction with each other. Today, in order for intricate scientific developments to reach their full capacity, a more interconnecting homogeneous interdependence of the various disciplines of the scientific world is required (Bertalanffy, 1968).

The world of science has come to acknowledge the reality of cross-discipline interdependence and interconnectedness. It has also become obvious that for this kind of discipline interdependence to function effectively, there has to be more interpersonal interaction and cooperation between the people who function within these systems (Davidson, 1983). Modern machines, such as the space age vehicle Apollo, are "user friendly" and capable of "interacting" with humans on a scale which up to now has been thought impossible. This interaction between developer (people) and the developed (machine) has also heightened our awareness of the need for the additional "interpersonal" variable to be part of the mix of "interdisciplinary" interdependence. It follows naturally that when we acknowledge the need for interdisciplinary dependence and consequent interpersonal interaction, that we necessarily involve other social realities such as socio/political/economic factors. In essence, it can be said that, in post modern scientific development (progress), we have a situation where no single discipline can function optimally without some interdependence on, and interconnectedness to, other disciplines and also the people who develop and operate them.

Through the introduction of the components of interdisciplinary dependency, interpersonal cooperation and socio/economic/political realities into post modern scientific discoveries and developments, it is no longer possible to view scientific development from an independent, isolated and mechanistic perspective. Science is now seen as operating within interdependent systems or disciplines. This systems, or holistic, approach makes possible the electronic/mechanical finesse that is evident in new age scientific breakthrough. The knowledge explosion and technological developments prevalent in post modern realities can no longer remain a number of small isolated inventions operating independently. They must now be seen as interconnecting and interdependent systems in their planning, arrangement and organization (Bertalanffy, 1968). This belief in the interdependence and the interconnectedness of scientific operations is the thesis which underpins the writings of systems theory put forward by Bertalanffy (1968), Ashby (1963), Ball (1978), and Walzlawick, Beavin and Jackson (1967). These writings advocate that nature operates through an interdependent network of "systems." Parts of a system are so interrelated to other parts that any change in one part will cause the total system to change. This systemic belief has moved our thinking away from the individualistic exclusive approach to both the physical and social sciences, and moved it towards an approach that is more open and inclusive. Systems theory has helped us come to the realization that all the so-called branches of science and consequent technology are somehow interconnected and interdependent. Boulding (1956) highlighted this sense of the inherent systems interconnectedness of disciplines by noting that nature did not invent academic disciplines, universities did. Bertalanffy (1968) stressed the interconnectedness and interrelatedness of all natural phenomenon. He believed that, if indeed the law of gravity applies equally to apples and the planets, and if the law of probability applies equally to genetics and life insurance, then laws of biological systems (i.e., living organisms are organized systems) should apply to the human psyche, social institutions and indeed to the whole global ecosphere. These biological systems, not unlike physical systems, are interactive and interdependent (Bertalanffy cited in Davidson, 1983).

A "system" can be any entity maintained by the mutual interaction of its parts. It is a set of interacting functional relationships that transform inputs into outputs (Stuart, 1980). It can be physical, like a television, or can be an organism interacting with the environment, like a person. A system is a whole that functions as a whole by virtue of the interaction of its parts. It is a bundle of interdependent and interacting relationships. For example, a watch functions as a system but is just a heap of parts if it is disassembled (Bertalanffy, 1968; Davidson, 1983; Stuart, 1980). Systemic thinking is premised on the notion that nature works not in isolated bits and pieces, but through a set of open systems and interdependent and interconnecting subsystems. Based on this premise, it is logical to assume that we cannot change or indeed interact with one system without impacting in some way on some other interrelated subsystem or system (Watzlawick, Beavin and Jackson, 1967).

When we picture the universe from a systems perspective, we begin to see the components that constitute the world around us as a holistic collection of interacting and co-dependent systems. The biologist, engineer, psychologist, chemist and sociologist operate as partners in their attempts to unravel the mysteries that surround the human condition. The solutions to human problems do not belong to one or another of these disciplines, but to the whole conglomerate working as a team.

According to systems theory, society functions as a "gestalt" or "holistic" entity. Social interaction is dependent on the interaction and interdependence of the systems operating within this whole. When we adopt this gestalt notion of how society functions, we also accept the premise that the whole is greater than the sum of all these interacting parts. This wholeness that results from the sum of parts is the cement which holds the systems together and is that which gives systems theory meaning. This gestalt or holistic force or what philosophers refer to as "the form" is only recognizable through the interactions within the systems, for example the interaction of students in a class or of members within a family group (Davidson, 1983). Our modern concept of marriage can be classed as a system in that marriage is more than just two persons being physically together, it is a relationship (the form) and it is the interaction and interdependence of both persons that makes the relationship functional. It is the emergence of this holistic magic or form that gives the marriage relationship its harmony (Davidson, 1983). A similar analogy can be made in relation to a symphony. It is the form, or that interconnectedness of the pieces, that make the symphony a cohesive listening experience. The poet laureate, Rabindranath Tagore (in Davidson, 1983), further accentuates the importance of seeing the totality or gestalt of something before we can fully appreciate its true meaning and beauty when he wrote: "by plucking her petals you do not gather the beauty of the flower."

Counselling from a Systems Perspective

Historically, counselling psychology has dealt with the resolution of problems through the process of working with the individual client. To a large extent this approach to counselling isolated the individual in the office of the psychologist and attempted to deal with the client's problems without referring to or including the impact of significant external forces such as family, work, etc. In this context, the main concern of counselling was what these external forces were doing to/for the client, and/or what the client was doing to/for them. Instead of involving significant others and/or groups in the healing process of the client, counsellors choose to talk about them as though they somehow were not relevant to the client's problems. Significant others and situations were not seen as "alive to the clients." Counsellors chose to omit from the process of counselling the very social systems that were quite possibly the cause of or at least related to the client's problems. Either way, an important element was missing from the counselling process, namely, the involvement of the interconnecting and interdependent systems.

Counselling psychologists, like other scientists, need to adopt a more systemic approach to their profession and begin to view the work they do with clients as more than just individual specific. There is evidence emerging within society and supported by the literature that the counsellor in the 21st century will need to be aware of and work with environments and not just with individuals (Johnson, 1990). When counselling individuals, counselling psychologists have to be aware of and gather the emergence of the totality of the client's life. That is, in order to fully understand and appreciate the client's difficulties, counsellors must be aware of the sum of the parts of the interconnecting systems (the environments) that impact on the client. The counsellor cannot appreciate or help bring about change to one part of the system, i.e., the client, without the knowledge and the cooperation of the other interconnecting systems and/or subsystems.

There is evidence that counselling psychologists, psychiatrists and social workers are beginning to use the systems approach in their work in dealing with human behavior problems (Ball, 1978; Satir, 1964, 1972; Lusterman, 1988; Johnson, 1990; Nichols & Everett, 1986). Given the realities of globalization and the general need for social interconnectedness today, counselling psychologists, to be effective, will have to adopt this systems approach in their counselling practice. No one is immune from the socio-political and socio-economic impact of our communication driven, global society with cyberspace telecommunication and rocket-driven transportation. The client and the counsellor cannot pretend to live in an environment that is immune and protected from these realities. Although the secrecy of the counsellor's office can be perceived as a safe haven for the revelation of the inner self, the reality of the impact of external socio/economic/political systems demands that any progress towards healing must take into account the social/economic systems in which clients live.

As counselling psychologists move slowly away from the isolated discipline-specific approach to their work, they have tended to go in one of two general directions. Some have opted for the interdisciplinary approach. Others, who have accepted the notion of the interdependence of social systems and sub-systems within society and their consequent impact on the lives of individuals, have adopted the systems approach in their counselling practice.

The systems approach to counselling has helped to bring the counselling practice from an emphasis on the intrapsychic, i.e., dealing with problems as if they only exist within the individual, to an emphasis on the interpsychic, that is, dealing with problems from the point of view of the real world context in which the client lives and works. Counselling psychologists who approach their practice from a systems perspective have become aware of the necessity of incorporating into their practice the interconnecting and interdependent systems that impact directly on their clients, for example, the family, school, church, peers, co-workers and the work place, etc. In this inclusive systems process, counsellors begin to see clients' problems more holistically. They no longer see problems as being solved in isolation and through exclusion, but through openness and inclusion. The home, work place, school and indeed, the community at large, all play a role in the therapeutic process. When counsellors acknowledge that the client is an integral part of an organized interdependent system and network of sub-systems, it changes their thinking about ways of dealing with problems and hence their approach to the counselling process.

The systems counsellor looks upon the presenting problems of the client not only as a dysfunction within the individual, but also as a dysfunction that is intricately enmeshed in the systems in which the client lives. This shifts the focus away from the intrapsychic processes of the client towards the interpsychic and interpersonal. The systems counsellor, while maintaining the individuality of the client as a specific system, goes beyond the individual and places the problem into the context of other systems such as the family, school, work place, etc. Placing the cause and possible solution of the client's problems in this broader social context is based on the belief that effective counselling not only depends on working with the individual, but to an equal degree, it depends on working with and understanding the many systems and subsystems in which the client lives and works.

There are basically two kinds of systems – open and closed (Vriend, 1985; Stuart, 1985). The systems counsellor works from the open model, which means that they are in constant interaction with the context in which the client lives. This open system acknowledges that clients are within themselves an integral system and thus, to a large extent, self-sustaining. At the same time, it believes that if this system is to function effectively, it must work and interact interdependently with other external systems. To bring about effective counselling, the counselling psychologist and the client must tap into these other systems and gather as much data as possible from them. This data can then be used as part of the planning strategy to help the client. Counselling from a systemic framework implies a gestalt mode of thinking on the part of the counsellor. A basic underlying assumption of the systems process is the belief that in order to help the client, the "whole" person must be understood. This wholeness can only be understood in terms of the relationship of the client with other impacting systems and vice versa. The client is only totally comprehended and hence more effectively helped when seen in the complete network of interacting systems in which s/he lives.

Although systemic counselling does retain some of the traditional one-on-one counselling, it is not married to that process. While it recognizes some of the traditional skills necessary for counselling like empathy, acceptance, warmth (Rogers, 1951), diagnoses, exploration, clarification and goal setting (Culley, 1991; Dixon and Glover, 1985), systemic counselling goes beyond these and explores and collects data from various outside entities or systems that effect the client. In doing this, the counsellor includes the total life of the client as an integral part of the counselling process. To do so not only avoids the trap of attempting to solve problems in isolation, but prevents the alienation of the significant others (systems) which the client needs for recovery support and in some cases for smooth "re-entry" into society.

As mentioned, there are two approaches made in counselling in its move to expand from the isolationist mode inherent in the one-on-one counselling process. Besides the systemic counselling approach, there is also the interdisciplinary process. This process is somewhat similar to systemic counselling insofar as it provides a forum whereby others, usually professionals from different specialties, come together to discuss the client. These professionals are usually from other disciplines of the helping professions, such as psychiatry, social work, medicine, education, etc. They come together to discuss, exchange professional ideas and diagnose the problems of a specific client. This process is not unlike placing the client in a fishbowl with each professional gazing at him/her without any interaction from the client. Besides diagnosing the problem, the interdisciplinary group often labels and prescribes solutions for the client's problems. Labelling the client and prescribing solutions often give the appearance of closure to the problem. However, these judgments are often made based on the strength of persuasion of the dominant discipline, without having any first hand knowledge of the client's problems and with only a superficial understanding of the systems which impact on the life of the client (Auserwald, 1966, p. 205). All too often clients are left to dangle at the diagnostic and labelling stage, without any further action as to what is to be done to help them.

In spite of its shortcomings, the interdisciplinary process is not without merit. It is at least an attempt to involve other professionals in the problem-solving process. However, from the client's point of view, he or she is still considered an isolated entity, operating in a vacuum without any connectedness to the systems in which they live. Professionals who come together for interdisciplinary conferences generally find it difficult to work out and/or carry out any long term plan for the client's improvement. One of the reasons for this impasse which so often occurs in the interdisciplinary process is the lack of trust and understanding and too often, the presence of petty professional jealousies that exist among the different professionals. Lack of openness and trust leads to a kind of professional protectionism. This protectiveness is very often made obvious and evident in the professional's slavish adherence to politically correct professional jargon. Such jargon inevitably gets in the way of clear communication among disciplines and is often used as a shield to protect and preserve what has been euphemistically referred to as "professional integrity." In reality, professional jargon is often no more than an attempt to hide ineptitude or to confuse consumers. In this consultative forum professional integrity often becomes so important that the needs of the client are sometimes forgotten and the preservation of the profession takes precedence. In many interdisciplinary meetings or case conferences, so much time is spent discussing the specific discipline system in which individual professionals find themselves that there is little time left for the client's problems and none for any meaningful consideration of the interconnecting systems which impact on them.

This preoccupation with their own specific professional integrity puts the interdisciplinary team at a great disadvantage. It blocks any form of meaningful discussion and hence understanding about the client and about the community systems in which the client lives. Consequently, the group fails to give or gain any real meaning and/or insight into the client's unique and personal experiences, and how these impact on or are impacted by the systems within which the client lives. A further weakness in the interdisciplinary approach is that the information (data) collected through this process tends to be defined more by what was said or done by a particular professional or group of professionals, rather than by an exploration of interrelated and interdependent systems and subsystems that give real meaning and focus to the life and problems of the client. This data, because of its source(s), is apt to be lacking in a very important informational ingredient, namely, the subtext or the hidden messages which are camouflaged just below the spoken words. These meanings are only available at the point of contact, both with the client and/or with the "systems" with whom the client interacts. This hidden or underlying data is very valuable and is only available to the counsellor who is willing and motivated to interact with all the systems which form part of the client's personal theory or belief system. The sometimes hidden agendas or sub-texts can supply invaluable information when helping clients deal with and understand their problems. The systemic counsellor can gather information or data that includes not only WHAT was said, but also, and more importantly, valuable insight into the WHYs and WHEREFOREs implicit in the WHAT.

Counsellors who adhere to systems counselling do not rule out completely the process of individual counselling or interdisciplinary consultation. However, they are not tied to these processes. The underlying thesis of the systems approach to counselling is that the best way to bring about attitudinal/behavioral change in an individual is to work through the interplay of the individual and the various systems in which s/he lives. What is missing from both the individual counselling approach and the interdisciplinary approach is a meaningful exploration of those interrelated and interdependent systems and subsystems. The systems counsellor gains most by extending his/her counselling practice to incorporate all of these systems.

Given the depth and scope of the systems approach to counselling, it is not surprising that it is widely used in such areas as family counselling. The systemic approach to family counselling is based on the belief that any problems experienced by one of the family unit must be seen to include the rest of the unit or the whole family, both immediate and extended. Data is gathered and action planned based on the observed interactions and reactions from all the systems involved, whether they be individuals such as a grandparent, or groups such as siblings. The process is based on the belief that the individual is interconnected to and indeed, a part of the family and the society in which s/he and the family lives. Hence, any change in the client will have to be reflected in these systems also. Meaningful intervention by the counsellor requires all these groups (systems) be included and involved in the counselling process (Driekurs, 1968; Adler, 1955; Satir, 1964, 1972; Kaslow, 1990; Lusterman, 1988; Grau, Moller and Gunnarsson, 1988; Nicholls & Everett, 1986).

Systems theory can be applied to counselling in multiple contexts or sites. For example, it can be applied in school counselling in a similar way that it has been adapted to family counselling. The school, like a family, is a system. It is not only a system unto itself, but consists of many sub-systems that constitute the whole process we call schooling. Within the system of the school, there exists the sub-systems of the administration, the teacher system and the student system. Impacting on these internal systems are the external administrative systems, which consist of parents, family, school councils, parent-teacher associations, the school board system, the government system and in some jurisdictions, the church systems. When we include the various associations or unions, we have quite a network of systems all imbued with one common purpose, namely the education of a child. Counselling psychologists who work in this quagmire of interconnected power brokers have to be able to see beyond the specific self of the individual when counselling a client. The reality is that this "one" client is a product of all these systems and must be seen in light of their interaction with and their impact on him/her and vice versa. Indeed, in this situation, it can be said that the client is greater than the sum of his/her parts. To truly understand the client in the school setting, counsellors have to be able to tap into all these systems for data that can be used to support both them and their clients in their counselling efforts. The student who presents with a problem is a product of this school environment and therefore must be seen as co-existing with it. The client's pain is also the system's pain and vice versa.

Most problems encountered by clients in school systems are engendered by friction among the many systems and sub-systems that exist within the school. This friction is the result of the client and the school clashing with one another over their individual needs and wants. For example, students can be at odds with teachers, parents and child can be at odds with the school or child and school may be at odds with the school board, or parent and school council at odds with the school principal. There can be any number of combinations of inter- and intra-systems dysfunction and often the client (student) is caught up somewhere in the works. In many instances, the problem for the clients (students) is that the school system is perceived by them as so overpowering, not only in its demands, but in sheer magnitude of size, that it tends to downplay any problem that the client may be experiencing. It is necessary therefore that, based on the notion of systemic counselling, all those involved in any way in the life of the client (student) should understand and appreciate the total school system's impact on the client. However, it is also important for them to know and understand that it (the school) is also one of "many" sub-systems that make up the total life of the client (student). When counsellors look at the student's/client's problems within the context of multifaceted systems, they can become aware of the "mortar" (the subtexts and hidden messages) that will add coherence and understanding to the client's problems.

Social systems, because they are made up of and hence manipulated by the human psyche, are subject to change. Because of the interdependence of one system on the other, any change in one is felt by the whole chain of systems. Any change in one member of a family system, for example, can effect that whole system, one member of a class of students who does not follow the rules of the class can have an impact on the whole class, and so forth. This systems interdependence can also be illustrated by looking within individuals as well. For example, when an individual experiences a headache, other parts of the body suffer besides the "head." The "head" ache can effect the emotional systems and the digestive systems and so forth. Similarly, in a systems approach to counselling, all sub-systems operating within and without the client are so interconnected that one cannot be changed in any way without having an effect on others. The counsellor using the systems approach must therefore be aware that all counselling interventions will impact somehow on others or other systems. Therefore they should be planned and executed with the needs of "all the individual systems" taken into account.

When other impacting systems are included in counselling, new insights are often gleaned about the individual that can greatly assist the counselling effort. For example, when other family or social systems are involved, the counsellor can often find within them people who are willing and indeed very capable of helping the client. These people can become, in many instances, part of the solution. They can work with the client in tasks that often do not require the professional intervention of the counsellor. This is particularly applicable to client problems that are home and school related. For example, parents and teachers can often do counselling-related work with students in the areas related to their learning. Teachers are, both theoretically and practically, masters in the area of learning and parents are often, with some help and encouragement, very good at helping to alleviate learning problems as they relate to behavior both in the school and in the home.

Using others within the client's systems to help the client does not necessarily imply establishing a traditional form of referral system. In actual fact using the systemic approach can prevent the "revolving door" trap of the "traditional" referral process. The traditional referral procedure usually consists of sending the client to another professional person and another and so on until the client revolves back to the original referral source. By using the systems approach, referrals, when judged necessary, are based on the concept of meaningful interaction within the system. Counsellors interact with significant others in the client's systems network. They gather information pertinent to the counselling process, right at source. Decisions as to who can best assist in the solutions to the client's problems are made at this interactive stage. The person to whom the client may be referred may not necessarily be a professional in the academic sense of the word. However, the person would necessarily be committed to the wellbeing of the client and be judged to be an effective intervener.

Systemic counselling looks at the problems of the client as falling within a much larger realm than simply the individual. It is community oriented and works on the premise that social relationships and interactions are an important part of the cause and the cure of the individual's problems. Like Jungian philosophy, it believes that the individual is a whole and not simply an assembly of parts. It also believes that the individual does not live or act in a vacuum, but is a living organism influenced and shaped to a large degree by the relationships and communication around him/her. The world of the client cannot be dissected into separate isolated bits and pieces. All these so-called bits and pieces are all intertwined, interconnected, interrelated and interdependent. Hence, clients cannot be effectively dealt with as if they were operating as separate from, and independent of these systems. The client is a totality of all that they have seen and been. The capital that the client brings to the counsellor's office is a conglomerate of all the psychological, cultural and social impingements that have entered his/her life. In order for the counsellor to fully understand the client, he/she must see the client in the light of the inherent dynamics of all these factors (Daniluk, 1989). In the systems approach, the emphasis is on the interdependence and interrelatedness of relationships between systems. It is through the therapeutic intervention into these interrelationships and systems that meaningful changes can be brought about and maintained in the client (Cottone, 1991).

Chapter 6
Career Counselling In the 21st Century

What made Shakespeare decide to become a playwright? Why did Elizabeth II ascend to the throne of England? Why did Ghandi accept the challenge of leadership for independence? We really do not know the answers to these questions. However, in the above cases, as in many others, we can find some meaningful answer by referring to the words of Shakespeare: "Some are born great, some achieve greatness, and some have greatness thrust upon 'em" (*Twelfth Night*, II:5). It is rare that any one decision or circumstance actually brings about our decision to enter into what society has termed a "career." Circumstance of birth, personality type, aptitudes and abilities all play a role in deciding what we choose as a career. We are also influenced in our career choice by the socio-economic, political and moral circumstances, either as they exist within the individual and/or as they operate within society in general. Therefore, the reasons for career choice include the client's personal attributes and factors such as the socio-economic and moral conditions that are prevalent in society. It is the combination of all these that act as determinants in the kind of work one chooses.

Beck (1992) delineates three stages in the development of work in society:
1. Work related to commodities textile production, circa 1918.
2. Work related to manufacturing, e.g., the auto industry and the use of oils as cheap energy, circa 1918-1981.
3. Technology related work, e.g., computer production and biotechnology, circa 1981.

This development from a textile/manufacturing to a high-technology work place has altered the work structure base of society and has brought about an enormous growth in jobs that require very different skills. This demand for continuous new and different skills in the work place has had a destabilizing effect on traditional patterns of career selection and on one's career life. These changes in the work place have led to a different emphasis on career education and career selection. For example, due to this rapidly expanding technology and its consequent impact on the work place, a person embarking on a career in the 21st century will likely make many career and job changes before retiring. This lack of stability and hence predictability in career patterns demands that clients be flexible in choice of career and be able to choose from and be successful at not one but many of these new and developing careers as they become available.

During the pre-industrial era, the social-political conditions were instrumental in the development of such careers as artisans, politicians, laborers, soldiers and clergymen, etc. In the industrial era, due to the advances made in the development of machinery, etc., wider career opportunities developed and such jobs as machinists and mechanics were added. In the present global age of technology and information (knowledge), coupled with different socio-economic and political conditions, many jobs of the pre-industrial and industrial times have been eliminated and new ones created (Beck, 1992). These new jobs have been and continue to be created out of an entirely different set of socio-economic needs, namely, information (knowledge) and technology.

The emphasis on technology and information has brought many obvious changes to the work place. For example, the office worker is no longer isolated from colleagues throughout the organization. Through the use of technologies such as e-mail, fax machines, etc., there is immediate interaction between various segments of the organization (Beck, 1992). This technology, although lessening the number of workers needed in the organization, at the same time opens up new job opportunities for those remaining. However, there are other, not so obvious trends and changes in society, either directly or indirectly related to technology, that also impact on the new reality of the world of work. Some of these are the growth of urbanization, the depletion of natural resources such as fish and forests, changes in family patterns, and the non gender specific reality of job selection. All of these have brought about extensive changes in the day-to-day life of the those who participate in the world of work and consequently have impacted on the approach that career counsellors take in their counselling.

Career counselling had its beginning in the early 20th century as a vocational placement movement. In the early 19th century, job placement was understood as the end or goal of what was called vocational guidance. Work was a thing to be done and had little to do with the measure of personal worth. Personal worth was defined by the monetary rewards of the job and not by the job itself. Consequently, job satisfaction was not as high on the priority list for workers as it is today. Today, work has a different meaning. Today we define ourselves by our work. It is no longer simply a means to an end (i.e., provision of basic needs), but rather an end in itself. Work today is seen as that entity in our lives that gives meaning to our very existence. This new and expanded meaning of work necessarily requires a new and expanded definition of what was once called vocational guidance and now referred to as career counselling.

This change in the meaning of work also impacted on the process of vocational guidance. The term vocational guidance changed to career guidance in the 40s and 50s and to career counselling in the 80s and 90s. This shift has meant more than the development of a new vocabulary. It has also brought with it a new process and philosophy regarding career counselling. Career counselling today means helping clients make career decisions that take on meanings above merely "getting jobs." It also incorporates the notion that work is related to self-esteem and considers a career as a life long and ever changing process. Career counselling has evolved to become the engine that drives the person to be always alert and ready to change jobs and/or drop into new work situations. Part of its mandate is to keep the person fuelled, i.e., in a state of developing, and hence a state of readiness to get involved in new careers either within or outside their chosen field. When we accept the reality that one's career is a factor in developing and maintaining self-esteem and identity and that it has to be built around the notion of change, planning and choice of career has to reflect this. Clients today must therefore be helped to accept changes in their career plan without seeing these change as a loss of, or as an affront to, their self-esteem or identity. It is therefore important that clients in career counselling are intellectually and psychologically prepared for the potential turmoil resulting from changes and movements within their chosen careers.

Career counsellors should help clients plan the future, knowing that changes will occur in the choices they make in the present. In order to do this effectively, career counsellors should be aware of the totality of experiences and education of their clients. This knowledge and experience constitutes the client's personal practical theory. It is their private, integrated, but ever-changing system of knowledge and experience that is relevant to situations at any time in their lives (Handal & Louvas, 1987). This practical theory, or what Rogers (1961) calls the phenomenal field or private life of the client, plays a major role in the kind of decisions that the client will make or be able to make. This is particularly true for people who are re-entering or changing occupations within the job market. The counsellor has to help clients bring to their reality all their personal and social experiences. In analyzing these attributes, clients will be able to understand from where they came, their abilities and potential abilities, and use these as a basis or stepping stone to better explore, accept and understand the next choice in their changing career patterns.

Besides taking into consideration the totality of experiences that the client brings to career counselling, the counsellor must also be aware of the rapidly changing economic and social base of post modern society. Career counsellors in the 21st century need to move their thinking away from the manufacturing based economy to the era of an economy that is based on technology and information. Because of this different economic base it is necessary that counsellors base career development (counselling) on the knowledge that the economy is no longer driven by large manufacturing plants or by mass use of natural resources. Rather, they should recognize that the engines that drive the economy today are in micro-businesses and single entrepreneurial ventures, e.g., computer manufacturing, small service industries and biotechnology (Beck, 1992). Coupled with this understanding should be the realization by client and counsellor that, because our society is information and technology driven and constantly changing, upgrading of skills is necessary throughout life. It is also important that counsellors be aware that in this new information and technology-based economy, there is instant information about ideas, goods and services from all over the world. The work place and the workers can no longer be viewed in terms of geographic isolation. As the nature of the social and economic structure of the globe changes, so too must workers be willing and able to change and develop their skills and work attitudes in order to keep pace with the changing global society.

The term globalization has been described by corporate researchers such as Ohmae (1989) and educational researchers such as Hargreaves (1994) as instant access to information about ideas, goods and services from all over the globe. This access to information is not limited to the network of electronic communications such as computer, the Internet or the visual/audio/print messages of television, but to actual physical interconnectedness as well. One only has to travel to places like China, Japan, Israel, Indonesia, the United States, Canada, Australia, Thailand, etc., and observe the masses of people from the various countries visiting and interacting with one another. We know, for example, that ten million Japanese travel outside their country every year. Easy access to previously inaccessible continents, brought on by swift and affordable jet travel, coupled with knowledge attained through television and the Internet, has made such intercontinental visitation a reality for people who some 20 years ago thought it impossible (Ohmal, 1989). During the 50s the growing intercommunication network around the earth led people to refer to the earth as the shrinking globe. Today, thanks to accelerated growth in the communication, telecommunication and transportation fields, we no longer refer to the earth as the shrinking globe. We are citizens of the world today and we are actually living in and experiencing the shrunken global world. We have been globalized, not necessarily by choice but by circumstance.

This fact of globalization has made us members of the new wave socio-economic society which Ohmae (1989) refers to as the ILE or the Interlinked Economy. The ILE as is presently constituted and, which in the main, consists of the Unites States, Canada, Japan and the European Community, and which will soon incorporate the growing economies of such places as Hong Kong, Taiwan and Singapore, is a powerful entity both from a socio-economic and socio-cultural point of view. The ILE has been created and continues to grow, based on the need for more liberal trading alliances. Free trading relations necessarily implies and requires a more closely knit interconnected socio-economic and cultural relationship (Ohmal, 1989). To survive in this interdependent milieu, we will need to have a greater understanding of all the different social, cultural, educational, political and working environments. To function economically in this interlinked economy requires workers to become aware of the realities and differences that exist among peoples of the different cultures. Clients in career counselling must be made aware of the varied and sometimes contradictory values that are part of cultures other than their own. This may necessitate learning to live with differences, letting go of some strongly-held values and adopting and/or adapting to those held by others. This implies not only changing the way they think, but more importantly, changing the way they do things. In reality this means adapting to the changes of the new age world or what has been called the global post modern world.

There are a number of implications for counsellors working with clients within the context of the global and technologically/information-driven world. Generally speaking, the major objective of career counselling is to help people make informed and realistic decisions regarding career patterns that they believe, based on the best available knowledge, will give them a productive life. Career counsellors should first and foremost be honest with clients and help them see career choice as a steady stream of decision making requiring a flexible approach to their career life. Career counselling should help clients continue with what may be difficult decisions in their future (Katz, 1987). This approach to decision making should therefore lay the foundation for a more open approach to future changes and developments in the client's careers. It is the ingredients of change and flexibility that differentiate the process of career counselling in the 21 st century from that of a decade ago.

In the practice of career counselling the counsellor plays a dual role. On the one hand, they are counsellors. This implies helping people come to an awareness, knowledge and understanding of self and how that self fits into the totality of their cultural, social and economic milieu. On the other hand, career counsellors are brokers of knowledge, well versed and up to date regarding the work place needs in the global post modern society. This necessitates an understanding of the socio-economic world in which the client lives and will live. Hence, it includes helping the client arrive at informed and reasonable career decisions for the present. However, given the economic and behavioral structure of post modern society, it also necessarily includes making clients aware that they have to be prepared to make career decisions throughout their lives. Because of the growing and ever-changing economic base that drives 20th and will continue to drive 21st century society, career decisions are not static but mutable and diversified. This necessarily suggests that career counselling must be seen in the context of "enabling" as opposed to "doing." Career counsellors have to enable clients to carry out the ongoing demands of career change.

To attend to this issue of change and flexible career planning for the post modern global work place, one question to be asked is, are we offering potential career counsellors opportunities for awareness and reflection and personal theoretical development that will help them come to an understanding and appreciation of their own particular cultural and work belief systems? It is only when career counsellors have a deep understanding and appreciation of their own socio-economic and cultural selves that they will be able to accept and understand the culture of others. To do this, we have to move away from a curriculum of studies for career counsellors that is insular, localized and nationalistic. Therefore, a broader curriculum that will take into account more than their own cultural world is needed. Curriculum for career education in the pre-global world was built on the notion of the meta-narrative and positivist philosophy. It was developed with a belief in scientific certitude and an adherence to traditional-based knowledge. Unquestioning belief in both these processes has been eroded somewhat today. Career education for counsellors in the global context must be based on the notion of inquiry, change and multi-culturalism. This approach cannot be based on absolutes within the intra-cultural milieu but has to concern itself with inter- and intracultural diversity and similarities.

The career counsellor has to be aware of the economic transformation that is taking place in the global society today. Bill Gates has replaced Henry Ford as the new guru of the present economy. Career counsellors have to move from thinking about careers in the manufacturing arena to careers in the technological areas. Being able to type is still an asset, but only a small part of the career in the computerized office. As Beck (1992) points out, many people make the mistake of taking high paying jobs that offer high salaries and perks. However, they should recognize that if these jobs are in the old dying economy, then they have a good chance of becoming trapped and without a future career. Counsellors have to be able to distinguish between careers that are survivors and those that are simply there but on the way out. Career counsellors should be careful and not prepare clients for careers that are rapidly becoming obsolete (Besk, 1992). Rifkin (1995) takes a pessimistic view of this decline in traditional jobs. He argues that after productivity drove young people from the farm, they came to the factory. They have since moved to the office. However, the new technology has driven them from the offices and there is now nowhere for them to go, hence there is an end to work as we know it. Drucker (1995) takes a more optimistic view of this movement, which he calls the age of social transformation. While he acknowledges that the job market is being inundated by revolutionary technological advancement and global competition, he believes that those who are ready (socially and educationally) for this change and willingly embrace it will prosper and those who are not will be left behind. There are losers and winners in this revolution of economic transformation. Education and career counselling are a key to being on the winning side (Rifkin, 1995).

Career counsellors should be at the forefront of the impact of the economic transformation and what the new economy needs in terms of readiness skills. However, counsellors need to recognize that even in the "new economy" there is still a place for basic skills. The three Rs are important. However, as Beck (1992) points out, the process of using them has changed. Part of the present career counsellors' store of knowledge has to be an understanding of what basic academic and social skills a client needs in order to function and grapple with the complexities of the 21st century global economy. Therefore, career counsellors have to be aware not only of the technical skills which the client needs to be employable in the new economy, but the social and academic skills needed as well. Similar skills as those developed in the pre-transformational society are still very useful. For example, the skills and professional knowledge learned in English or Social Work are still important, but they must be applied in different ways and in different settings. English skills can be used in such things as translating software manuals and our social work skills can be used more and more in eldercare (Beck, 1995).

It is clear that the current understanding of a career connects with the client's self-esteem and identity. Choosing a career today is a personal and dynamic endeavor through which one constantly recreates oneself in a global, competitive and interactive society. With this continuous development of technologies in the global society, those planning a career must realize that their place of work may not be confined to one place or indeed one country. With the rapid growth and development of electronic communication, the work place as we know it today, that is, major offices housed in multi-storied complexes, may be substituted in the future with a sophisticated electronically equipped home office. To survive this move to a techno-globalized world, worker's skills, academic and social and technical, need to be constantly renewed and upgraded if they are to be saleable in the post modern work place.

Career counselling in these changing times and environments is not an easy task. The very definition of career counselling used in the past may not fit the present. The world of occupations is no longer seen as a constant; consequently, the definition of career counselling is not a constant. Therefore, within this global ever-changing economic milieu, counsellors engaged in career counselling need to rethink their definition of career counselling. Such a definition of career counselling has to incorporate the reality of the work ethic and social structure of work in the 2000s. Srebalus et al. (1982) define career development as a system that identifies, describes and interrelates important factors affecting lifelong human involvement in work. Today, the notion of lifelong involvement with work goes beyond merely getting a job or changing from one job to another. It implies a continuous involvement in career decision making throughout one's work life. This change in career development is particularly true for workers employed in the old economy based on manufacturing. These workers have to be able and willing to make the crossover from the old economy to the new economy. That is to say, the client must be "helped" into the era of the computer and its concomitant technologies. Those with the new technologies are replacing the one time "skilled" worker of the 50s. Without a commitment to retrain and make new career decisions, the present or beginning worker may remain in the unemployable group as the new economy marches forward. Technology has gone from being a tool that workers use to the driving engine that is a doer in its own right (Beck, 1992). To be skilled in the new economy, workers must catch up with technological progress and harness it so that it will bring them to new levels of skill previously unknown.

While redefining career counselling within the context of this global and ever-changing socio-economic milieu of the 21st century, counsellors have to be careful not to simply throw away what is valuable from the 20th century. For example, Parsons (1908) developed a definition of career counselling using three factors: (1) a clear understanding of yourself, your aptitudes, resources, limitations and their causes; (2) a knowledge of the requirements and conditions for success, advantages and disadvantages of compensation, opportunities and prospects in different lines of work; (3) true reasoning on the relations of these two groups of facts. Parsons is saying that to make a decision regarding vocational choice (career choice), a counsellor has to help clients know themselves, understand the engines that drive the economy and come up with choices based on these two. This definition of career counselling can easily be adapted into the 21st century definition of career counselling. However, given the nature of the global economy today, we can add a fourth factor, namely, the need for the client to be flexible and recognize that choices made today will not last a lifetime. Present day choices made in a global interlinked job market without geographic boundaries, in a specific geographic centre, could merely be a bridge to another choice at another location. With this in mind, I would propose the following as a working definition of career counselling:

> *A process whereby the client comes to an honest understanding and acceptance of the various personal attributes that constitute self. In tandem with this process, the client should have the opportunity, through the counselling process, to be cognizant of the personal, social and educational barriers prevalent in the work place; become fully aware and versed in the knowledge and understanding of the techno-educational skills and personal qualities needed to enter the work place, and realize that flexibility is essential in order to become and remain productive in the new techno-social economy of the 21st century.*

It can be said that the current understanding of a career connects with the client's self-esteem and identity. Choosing a career is a dynamic, personal and social endeavor through which one is constantly recreated in order to compete in a global, competitive and interactive society. The rapid growth and development of electronic communication in the work place as we presently experience it, is indeed metamorphic and confusing. Because of the continuous development of technologies in the global society, those planning a career must realize that their place of work may not be confined to one place or indeed one country. Also, major offices housed in multi-storied complexes may be substituted with a sophisticated electronically equipped home office. Therefore, to survive this move to a techno-globalized world, workers' academic and technical skills need to be in a constant state of renewal and upgrading and their social/political awareness skills need to be polished and developed if they are to survive and prosper in the post modern global work place.

Chapter 7
Career Counselling Young Women

When one looks at career counselling, two themes overall become evident. First of all, it is clear that the current understanding of a career connects with a person's self-esteem and identity. Secondly, with the continuous development of technologies in a global society, those seeking a career must realize that their skills need constant upgrading in order to ensure themselves a place in a very dynamic and ever-changing work world. Consequently, choosing a career in today's world, although a personal decision, involves an ongoing recreation of oneself which is greatly influenced by a competitive and interacting society. These realities are particularly evident when one considers issues of gender as impacted by the world of work. Gender issues in the work world have many implications for career counsellors.

The 70s and early 80s saw the rise of the women's movement and an acknowledgment by society of gender discrimination in the work place. As women began their journey towards self-discovery and independence, career counselling for female clients grew into a distinct form of counselling. As a result, any examination of career counselling must include an understanding of this psycho-socio-economic transformation, both in society in general and in the work place in particular.

In modern society, career choice was divided along gender lines. This was a simple process and simplified the social order by nicely dividing the work place into men's work and women's work. However, there was one major flaw – the division of labor lacked the basic principle of equality. Women were restricted in their choices of careers, mainly due to society's traditional male-dominated gender values.

The struggle by women for their place as equal workers in the work place has brought with it a whole range of special counselling needs, which were heretofore not part of counsellor's repertoire. This need to transform counselling attitudes came about from the fact that women were demanding an end to discrimination at work. Women were also demanding that people, particularly career counsellors, show an understanding of their career development and career needs as being no less equal to and indeed no different from men's. This new demand challenged both female and male counsellors to face their own gender biases and to help women achieve equal opportunity in the work place.

Career counsellors on the eve of the new millennium are still faced with similar difficulties. Although it would appear that gender equality in the work place is now, in theory at least, accepted, in fact there is a comfortable fiction that this ideal has practically been attained. Women are working in jobs which were previously closed to them. Some women are making incredibly high salaries. The idea that a husband won't let his wife work is almost obsolete (Collier, 1982). However, the truth is that women's difficulties in the world of work have simply become more subtle; they are by no means gone. Career counsellors therefore must become even more sensitive to bias against their female clients, both in the work force and in their own counselling.

In order to give women full and effective career counselling, counsellors must remain informed about the current situation of women in the work force. As this is such a rapidly changing area, counsellors can never assume that their understanding is complete. It is essential that they continually and consciously seek out information on women and work. It is a counsellor's responsibility to stay abreast of the social indicators, demographic data and employment statistics to understand change and trends in the work force. He or she should also seek to understand the many barriers, both internal and external, which may impede a woman's success.

Knowledge and understanding of the facts about women and work can help a career counsellor in two ways. Firstly, these facts can help break down myths and bias in the counsellor's own mind. They can help him or her acknowledge the realities of working women's lives. Secondly, but equally important, the facts can do the same thing for the clients. Women tend to use myths to discriminate against themselves, especially in the area of work and achievement. What society as a whole believes, women also tend to believe, even when it is to their personal disadvantage (Collier, 1982). It has been suggested that the best possibility for destroying such destructive myths is through presentation of fact rather than through argument. One useful method is to present to women the realities of the work world through a fact sheet (Collier, 1982).

Women are working more than ever before, making up approximately 50% of the work force. However, women are still earning less than men for equal jobs. Although individual women have made gains in various professions, women as a group remain dramatically poorer and more economically vulnerable than men. The ratio of men's to women's wages for full-time, year-round work has averaged about 60% for several decades (Hansford, 1988). One of the major reasons for this wage gap is that, although the numbers of female workers are increasing, many of those workers remain clustered in jobs traditionally thought of as feminine, such as secretaries, cashiers, bookkeepers, nurses, waitresses, elementary school teachers, nursing aides, sales workers, sales supervisors, typists, etc. The vast majority of jobs in the higher-paying professional occupations are still held by men (Collier, 1982; Ehrhart & Sandler, 1987).

Of course, women do not work in a vacuum. Social factors play a large role in determining women's career development. For instance, women are working more than ever before because of unprecedented economic necessity: Women are staying single longer, divorce is more common, and child support is mainly the woman's burden. Counsellors must remember that, for women as much as for men, work is a matter of economic survival. They must also take into account the double workload of most working women. In addition to their careers, most women are still doing most of the unpaid "women's work" – child-rearing and housekeeping. Even in dual-worker couples, women perform 75% of this work (Wolf, 1990; Collier, 1982). In fact, women are often expected to sacrifice their own careers to their children's and their husband's needs (Cook, 1993). They often leave their jobs to raise their children or to follow their husband's career moves. This creates an intermittent work pattern, making it difficult for women to advance in their career development (Cook, 1993).

Women's participation in the labor force differs radically from men's. Both counsellors and clients must be aware of these facts in order to help women make informed career choices. However, a career counsellor's responsibility goes well beyond showing his or her female clients that they may be entering the work force at a disadvantage. Presenting the facts must include giving women positive information on a wide range of career possibilities, including those which have traditionally been restricted to men. Studies show that women tend to narrow their options and often remain relatively passive in regard to work and income (Collier, 1982). Access to information gives women considerably more power (and probably less conventionality) in their career choices.

Career counsellors must make available to their clients materials which inform, encourage and support women in their career development. The amount of informational material which supports the occupational integration of women is growing (Report of the Collaborative Action Working Group, 1988). Counselling materials should be such as to encourage women to participate in all areas of training and employment. They should demonstrate that women are capable and do succeed despite the difficulties that they face in the working world (Report of the Collaborative Action Working Group, 1988). Unfortunately, not all women can simply take available information and apply it to their lives. Barriers, such as lack of confidence or discrimination, may make it difficult for them to use the information in a practical way. A career counsellor must understand how these barriers, which may be either internal or external, may impede his or her clients' achievement.

During sex-role socialization, many women develop "feminine" characteristics which act as internal barriers to their career success. These characteristics are often reinforced by family, friends, school, community and the media. Some of these internal barriers are that women tend to engage in less long-term planning than men, women tend to be unclear about their wants and needs, women tend to depend on others to make decisions, women tend to gain self-esteem through the achievements of significant others, women tend to nurture others at their own expense and women tend to mistrust their ability to determine their own futures. To remain feeling fully feminine, women often lower their own aspirations, expect less of themselves than men and experience more confusion than men regarding the importance of achievement in their lives (Collier, 1982, p. 139).

Counsellors must clearly understand, however, that to acknowledge that women may impede their own achievement is not to blame the victim (Collier, 1982). A lack of achievement is not natural to women, it is a learned behavior which can be changed. Environments often present individuals with certain opportunities, expectations, demands and rewards based on their biological sex. Thus, many male/female differences tend to be highly influenced by the situation, rather than rigidly programmed within the individual (Cook, 1993).

Career counsellors can help women surmount these internal obstacles to their success. First of all, they must make it clear that these are learned behaviors. The client should examine the system of feedback and rewards which caused her to adopt attitudes which inhibit her achievement. This brings the barriers into consciousness where they can be challenged. Since many women lack self-confidence with regard to work, it is important that the counsellor reassure the client that she is not personally inadequate. The client must learn to accept responsibility for her own situation. If the counsellor makes a woman's choices for her, he or she is simply repeating the social pattern which hurts so many women in the first place (Collier, 1982). Finally, specific projects, such as formulating a career plan, can give women a sense of power and reward them for positive action.

There are also external barriers in the world of work which are specific to women. These exist in society's attitudes towards working women and in the structure of the working world. Although open discrimination against women is becoming less common, there are still many people and practices in the work place which, consciously or unconsciously, affect equality. Career counsellors should be aware of the existence of these barriers and help their female clients assert their rights to equal opportunity, equal treatment and equal pay. Often women, because of their socialization, do not insist upon their legal rights, or demand that their special needs be understood. In such situations the counsellor should be able to help them learn what their rights are and to take the necessary steps to act on them.

Not all women have equal opportunity in the work force – in some cases even before they are hired. Some employers are hesitant to hire a woman for a non-traditional job. Others will hesitate to hire a woman who has children, believing that her role as a mother will detract from her paid work. Counsellors should let their women clients know that such discrimination in the hiring process is illegal.

Another area where many women experience discrimination is in their wages. As stated earlier, women earn approximately 60 cents for every dollar earned by men. This wage gap exists because occupations which are dominated by women, such as clerical and sales work, tend to be valued less and consequently paid less than comparable occupations dominated by men (i.e. machine operation). In recent years there has been a new recognition of the importance of equal pay for work of equal value. Currently, under the Canadian Human Rights Act, it is discriminatory practice for an employer to establish or maintain differences in wages between male and female employees employed in the same establishment who are performing work of equal value. This means that predominantly female jobs can be compared with predominantly male jobs in terms of skill, responsibility, effort and working conditions. Career counsellors should explain this right to their female clients and, if the client wishes, help them to act on it.

One of the most underacknowledged forms of discrimination women may encounter in the work place is sexual harassment. Studies show that 70%-88% of women will be harassed in their working lives. Sexual harassment is defined as "any unwelcome sexual advances, requests for sexual favors, unnecessary touching or patting, suggestive remarks or other verbal abuse, leering at a person's body, compromising invitations, physical assault and other verbal or physical conduct of a sexual nature directed at an individual(s) by a person who knows or ought reasonably to know that such attention is unwanted" (Sexual Harassment Board, 1992). The Newfoundland Federation of Labour (1982) further related harassment to career equality by defining it as "any sexually-oriented practice that endangers a woman's job, that undermines her job performance, and threatens her economic livelihood."

Sexual harassment is not always treated as a serious problem. In some instances, women are often blamed or blame themselves for the harassment. Career counsellors must assure women who are being harassed that they are victims of a legal offense and that there are steps that they can take to stop it. The counsellor should encourage the client to confront her harasser directly. If the harassment continues, the counsellor should help the woman to document all incidents of harassment. She can use this documentation as evidence when she takes further action. The next step is for the woman to speak to the harasser's supervisor and present him or her with this evidence. If even this fails to stop the harassment, then the counsellor should encourage the client to take legal action. Section 13.1(2) of the Canadian Human Rights Act prohibits sexual harassment. The Newfoundland Human Rights Code also has provisions respecting sexual harassment and a complaint may be made to the Human Rights Commission, who will investigate.

Some of the barriers to equality for working women are firmly rooted in the structure of the working world. Part of the reason for this is that the work force has long been dominated by men. Due to their own socialization programs, males reflect a value that is more traditional and a reflection of male values and needs. These values of the work place assume that working is the primary role in a person's life (Collier, 1982). Yet, because of women's multiple roles – worker, mother, housekeeper – this kind of commitment is often impossible. Women must often choose not to work or not to have children, to fill both roles (often a source of great stress), to work part time at low wages or to work intermittently (Collier, 1982). Individually, career counsellors must help women deal with these choices. Collectively, however, counsellors can work to change labor practices and the community's degree of support for family life through community action.

This book emphasizes the fact that a counsellor's practices must be guided by a personal counselling philosophy or theory that is informed by a body of knowledge and research and influenced by the context in which counselling is practiced. Thus far, this chapter has placed its emphasis on the practical aspects of career counselling for women – what a counsellor should specifically do. However, in order for these practices to be meaningful, a counsellor should develop a personal theory based on the reality of the need for empowerment of women and an end to discrimination (based on the reality of the psycho-socio-economic realties of both society and the work place). In this sense, career counselling of women can be seen as a quasi-political activity. Career counsellors working with women must realize that for every act which takes place in a counselling session, there is a parallel political consequence in the world. For instance, if a woman lacks self-esteem at work, it may be because she has been personally mistreated in the work place. In helping this individual woman find her personal power, the counsellor could be involved with issues of inequality and/or discrimination.

In order to further explore the link between counselling and political philosophy, one can look to the area of feminist counselling. Feminist counsellors have made this link the basis of their work with their clients. Feminist counselling first began in the late 60s and early 70s, when many women in the counselling profession began to recognize a conflict between the popular psychological theories which they had learned and their experiences as women. Encouraged by the growing strength of the women's movement, these counsellors went on to form a women's alternative to mainstream therapy. Feminist counsellors are women who use their counselling skills primarily to help other women, and whose practices respect and reflect feminist consciousness. Like other counsellors, feminist counsellors come from many different backgrounds and base their work in many different theoretical orientations. However, all of them "bring to their work a consciousness about women's common oppression, a consciousness about the oppression of particular minority groups within the larger female population, an understanding of the psychological effects on women of their oppression, a knowledge of how to work with the particular problems experienced by women, and a belief in their client's expertise" (Laidlaw & Malmo, 1991, p. 397).

Feminist counsellors do not believe in labelling their clients as sick, or in blaming them for their problems. Rather, feminists believe that the great majority of women with psychological problems are reacting to unhealthy and destructive circumstances in their lives, both past and present, and have developed unhealthy coping strategies. Rather than helping the women to adjust to these circumstances, feminists are committed to helping their clients change them (Laidlaw & Malmo, 1991). Feminist counselling links the personal and political in women's lives, showing them how feminism relates to their personal struggles. According to Levine (1980) feminist counselling is an approach that is based on the premise that women have a vested interest in and also the potential to change what is, both for themselves and other women. In this process women can reclaim the strength and power and talent that is within them. This point is also implicit in the writings of such feminist family counselling researchers as Luepnitz (1988), Goldner (1985), Hare-Mustin (1994).

On a practical level, feminist counselling is based on a supportive egalitarian relationship between the counsellor and the client. As Laidlaw and Malmo (1991) point out, the feminist counsellor introduces herself by her first name, stepping out of professional neutrality. When appropriate, she shares stories of her own experience. She also consciously avoids judging or labelling the client. The client is encouraged to take an active role in choosing the counsellor that is best for her, and in deciding the content of her counselling sessions (p. 398). While the counsellor has certain expertise in therapeutic techniques, the client is believed to be her own best expert on her own life, and to be capable of finding her own solutions (Lewis, 1992).

Biases in Career Counselling

Career counsellors have the potential to play an important role in helping women to achieve career equality. Unfortunately, however, they sometimes do just the opposite. Rather than break down barriers for women, some counsellors act as barriers themselves. Griffiths (1994) suggests that women are often locked into low-paying jobs by virtue of their educational level, the type of counselling they receive and society's unwillingness to accept the real reasons why women work. In 1988, The Report of the Collaborative Action Working Group on Counselling affirmed that employment counselling can act as a barrier to women's labor equality. Despite the outpouring of information on the counselling of women since then, this remains a problem.

It is no surprise that sexism exists in the discipline of career counsellors. Counsellors are as vulnerable as other people to the myths and bias about men and women that pervade our society. Research has shown that both male and female counsellors have different career expectations for male and female clients. Broverman et al. (197) noted that counsellors equate the definitions of psychologically healthy men and healthy adults. However, their definition of a healthy woman is not that of a healthy adult. Buczek (1981), cited in Robinson and Page (1988), found that women clients are more likely to have "social concerns," while underestimating their professional and vocational concerns.

Many counsellors tend to label different careers as either masculine or feminine. Hopkins-Best (1987) conducted a survey of 4 secondary level school counsellors to see if their agreement as to the appropriateness of various career goals for a student would differ as a function of the student's sex. She found that there was significantly higher agreement among the counsellors that semi-skilled (rather than professional) jobs were more appropriate for female students. As well, traditionally male-dominated occupations (i.e., military service, apprentice, electrician, etc.) were rated as more appropriate for male students. Traditionally female-dominated occupations (i.e., receptionist, beautician, teacher's aide, etc.) were rated as more appropriate for female students.

Sex norms such as these have long limited women's opportunities and career counsellors need to work to remove them from their counselling processes and materials. Studies have shown that when a student is establishing post-secondary goals, a significant other's agreement or disagreement can influence their aspirations (Hopkins-Best, 1987). Counsellors are an example of a significant other and they have a responsibility not to limit their client's futures. All clients have the right to full and fair career counselling. Counsellors must be aware of their own values and biases and the effect that these may have on their female clients. In doing this, it is often invaluable for a counsellor to seek out the knowledge and perspective of other professionals. Participation in professional development programs, consultation and/or supervision can help counsellors to better monitor their activities and materials, ensuring that they are expanding rather than limiting their clients' potential.

Guidelines for Career Counsellors

Thus far in this chapter I have outlined a number of broad recommendations for career counsellors of the new millennium. However, it may also be helpful to provide a short and specific list of guidelines for career counsellors. Counsellors can use this list to evaluate the progress of their own counselling, and decide which areas of it need to be reconsidered.

The following list was compiled by The Collaborative Working Group on Counselling in 1988. This group was formed by the First Ministers of Canada who, in 1986, decided that career counselling was a structural barrier to women's equality. The Working Group recommended that individuals involved in career counselling with girls and women adhere to the following guidelines:

1. Counsellors are aware of the assumptions underlying various theoretical approaches to the practice of career counselling and recognize that such theories may apply differently to women and men. Counsellors continue to examine theoretical biases and assumptions underlying their practice to ensure that they utilize theories and models which are free of sex bias and sex role stereotypes and promote the realization of full potential by girls and women.

2. Counsellors ascribe no preconceived limitations on the direction or nature of potential changes or goals in counselling with women. In particular, counsellors ensure that career choice is an open process and that no individual is limited by gender – or by race, age, disability, ethnicity, sexual orientation or religion – from the exploration of any career option.

3. Recognizing that the use of male terms as gender-neutral reflects bias against women, counsellors use inclusive and gender-fair language in all oral and written communication and ensure that resources used to assist clients with decision-making are gender-fair. As an extension of this principle, counsellors also avoid the use of generic adjectives to describe women with handicaps (e.g., blind, deaf and so forth) in order to avoid excessive focus on the disability; descriptive phrases (e.g., women with visual handicaps) are used as a much-preferred alternative to the more generic adjectives.

4. Counsellors are knowledgeable about support services available to women (e.g., child care, legal aid, health care, transportation, emergency services) and assist clients in accessing community resources which are suited to their needs. Where significant gaps are identified in support services available to women, counsellors may initiate or act as catalysts for the development of such support systems in their communities.

5. Counsellors continue throughout their professional careers to gain knowledge and awareness of social, biological and psychological influences on female development in general and their career development in particular. As part of their ongoing professional development, counsellors continue to inform themselves about specific issues which may have an impact on the career decision-making of girls/women, e.g., balancing vocational and family roles, issues related to training and employment of women in non-traditional occupations, family violence, sexual harassment and sexual assault, as well as acquiring knowledge which is relevant to counselling particular sub-groups, such as women with disabilities, women who are culturally different, long-term welfare recipients and female offenders.

6. Counsellors understand that the source of client difficulties often rests not only in the woman herself, but also in situational or cultural factors which limit her concept of self, her aspirations and the opportunities available to her. Counsellors recognize and are sensitive to the effects of stereotyping, prejudice and discrimination on the basis of gender – as well as race, age, disability, ethnicity, sexual orientation and religion – and work to counteract the negative effects of such attitudes and actions.
7. Counsellors are aware of and constantly review their own values and biases and the effects of these on their female clients. Counsellors assess and monitor their own activities to ensure gender-fair practices, as well as participating in professional development programs, consultation and/or supervision to assist in identifying and working through personal biases and issues which have a limiting effect on their work with female clients.
8. Counsellors support the elimination of sex bias within institutions and individuals, by promoting fair and equal treatment of all individuals through services, programs, theories, practices and treatment of colleagues and clients which recognize the full potential of each.
9. Recognizing that there are circumstances where clients will have a preference for a same or opposite sex counsellor, whenever possible, clients will be given the opportunity to choose the counsellor with whom they work.

Of course, the career counselling of women, like all areas of counselling, can be carried out the most effectively and efficiently when fully supported by the hiring institution or jurisdiction. Therefore, hiring agencies have a responsibility to promote the full and equal participation of girls and women in the labor force. To this aim, The Report of the Collaborative Working Group on Counselling suggests that these agencies should make the following commitments:

a. to provide continuing professional development and training opportunities to those who counsel girls and women.
b. to ensure that all communications and resource materials used and/or produced within an institution/jurisdiction use gender-fair and inclusive language.
c. to provide counsellors with information on the full range of support systems available to girls and women.
d. to provide information on the full range of career choices to girls and women.
e. to provide girls and women with their choice of counsellor (male or female) whenever
f. to establish a review process to ensure that career counselling services for girls and women promote the occupational integration of girls and women.

This chapter has made some suggestions to those concerned with the career counselling of women in the new millennium. However, this is only the briefest of overviews of a field which is constantly growing and changing. Thus, it is every career counsellor's responsibility to regularly seek out new information on the counselling of women (Hoyt, 1989). Robinson and Page (1988) suggest that it is the responsibility of the counsellor to help the woman client: ". . . develop and maximize her own autonomy, academic skills, and self-growth, as well as to exercise choice about her personal and professional future, while at the same time, not unfairly condemning or denigrating choices or behaviors which happen to be consistent with traditional gender stereotypes" (p. 100). However, change in society makes it an area where the counsellor can take nothing for granted, where habits and routines must constantly be questioned in light of the facts (Collier, 1982). Counsellors, therefore, need to not only develop their self-awareness of the difficulties that surround female counselling, but also keep abreast of current literature and research in the area. As Collier (1982) points out "there is certainly some truth to the joke that counselling a working woman is almost as hard as being one" (p. 151).

Chapter 8
Legal and Ethical Issues in Counselling Psychology

Post modern society, because of its penchant for change and uncertainty, is fraught with confusion and imbalance. This disequilibrium effects all the threads of our social fabric, particularly those related to ethical and moral rights and responsibilities. For example, when there is an ethical question which involves coming down either on the side of the individual or the society, there is vacillation – on the one hand there is the tendency to show a great concern for the rights of the individual, while at the same time, there is the equally strong belief in the common good or the rights of the community over the rights of the individual. This dilemma often precipitates a general lack of trust and confusion. Therefore it enhances the desire for individuals and groups to challenge their individual and collective rights to a degree unknown in history. Herlihy and Sheeley (1988) describe this present social/legal/ethical climate by pointing out that we live in a litigious society, with an ever-growing attitude that if someone is injured, then someone must pay.

In light of this kind of social climate, the helping professions without exception, are concerned both collectively and individually with ethical and legal issues. Most have attempted at least to develop some specific codes of ethics. Blackham (1974) defines codes of ethics as attempts to ensure that counselling is done within the framework of moral responsibility: responsibility means a liability to be called to account, and to have behaved responsibly is to be able to justify oneself when called to account. Cooper (1992) suggests that it is the function of ethics to control the behaviors of practitioners by attempting to ensure that behaviors accord with the beliefs underlying the establishment of the codes.

As the need for counselling psychology in post modern society becomes more and more pronounced, and because of the uncertain social conditions in which counsellors work, counsellors are continually confronted with questions regarding ethical and legal situations which occur in their practice. Hence, there is a pressing need for counsellors to become knowledgeable about the ethical and legal responsibilities of their profession. Cohen (1992) emphasizes the importance for counsellors to become familiar with what is considered legal and illegal in their practice. This is true not only from a professional development point of view, but also for their own protection.

Counsellors, not unlike any other professionals, cannot plead ignorance of the law as an excuse for not upholding it.

This lack of understanding and study of ethical issues reiterates the concern voiced by Brammer & Shostrom (1968), who suggested at that time that the most important safeguard against unethical behavior is knowledge and experience. Gross & Robinson (1985) further emphasize this point by stressing the importance of providing the beginning professionals with information and training regarding concepts, theories, models and procedures to be used in the effective implementation of consulting practices. These, they point out, can be found in the textbooks, workshops, articles and curricular offerings of programs.

Counselling psychologists, like other professionals, are liable for their actions. Ignorance of the law is no excuse for unethical or illegal behavior. Lack of knowledge and understanding on the part of counsellors of their ethical responsibility is borne out in the results of a United States national study of department heads in counsellor education by Stadler & Paul (1986). This study found that 75% of the respondents had no formal course work in professional ethics as part of their graduate training program. Either ethics was not addressed at all in their program, or it was addressed indirectly through informal coursework. It was also found in this study that ethics-related discussions frequently take place only when a student or faculty member identifies an issue as an ethical one.

There is a strong and continuously growing demand for counselling today. This demand places the responsibility on the counsellor to be professionally prepared to deal with the issues that arise in their counselling practice. However, given the strong awareness and desire on the part of clients to be ethically and legally satisfied, it is incumbent on counsellors and counsellor educators to ensure that counsellors receive at least minimum training in ethical and legal issues at their graduate level of education. The following is a brief survey of some of the more prominent and pressing ethical and legal issues of concern for counsellors both now and into the 21st century.

The Process of Making Ethical Decisions

Ethical decision making, like decision making in general, takes into account many factors, such as the social conditions which impinge on the outcome of the decision and the effects of the outcome on self or other individuals, etc. Ethical decision making follows a similar pattern and is concerned with the outcome of the decision as it affects the client, the professional, significant others in the life of the client and good versus not good outcomes, etc. A number of authors have put forth theories of ethical decision making that outline firm, yet general frameworks for the ethical decision-making process (Rest, 1979; Stadler, 1985; The Canadian Psychology Association, 1988). Schultz (1991) developed from these theories a comprehensive and succinct model which he calls the Integrative Approach. Counsellors would do well to examine these theories before beginning their counselling careers. As a collage of theories (models), these provide very useful theoretical and practical suggestions as to what ought to be considered by counsellors as they work through the various steps of the ethical decision-making process.

Confidentiality and Privileged Communication

Confidentiality and privileged communication are two areas which create ethical dilemmas frequently faced by counselling psychologists. These dilemmas put the onus on counsellors not only to be familiar with the limitations of disclosure, but also to explain these limits to clients. Privileged communication suggests that the counsellor is legally bound to keep information confidential. That is to say the information received by the counsellor in guaranteed under the law to remain confidential. This applies most commonly between husband and wife, attorney and client, and clergy and penitent (McCarthy & Sorenson, 1993). However, both Sheeley and Herlihy (1989) and Morse (1990), cited in McCarthy and Sorenson (1993), point out that there are now a number of states in the United States where the law of privileged communication between client and counsellor apply either in part or in full (as far as I can ascertain, there are no such laws in any province in Canada).

Confidentiality, on the other hand, is not legally binding, therefore there are many "grey areas" of ethics to be considered by the counsellor when accepting a client for counselling. Consequently, during the first interview, there ought to be a clear and candid discussion between the client and counsellor regarding the limits that may exist with respect to any confidences that may be communicated during the interview (Keith-Spiegel & Koocher, 1985). By providing such information early, it is possible for both the client and the counsellor to prevent problems from happening later on. This point is further stressed by Davis & Ritchie (1993) in so far as they suggest that informed written consent should be secured from the client dealing with limitations of confidentiality. They cite the example of a counsellor being required to report suspected child abuse. If the client should make this disclosure to the counsellor, then this information could not be kept confidential. The client therefore needs to know that there is a mandate on the part of the counsellor to report this information and that it is illegal for the counsellor to withhold it. However, Tompkins and Melving (1993) point out that although generally the law takes the position that, when necessary, courts are privy to all private conversations, however, the law sets about to specifically exclude those communications in which the court's right to know is outweighed by the sanctity of the relationship (p. 336). They do suggest, however, that counsellors should maintain carefully written and thorough notes which document any discussions of issues such as confidentiality, the need to protect third parties and informed consent. It is suggested that counsellors also maintain private notes that may not be subject to judicial scrutiny. This practice of note or record keeping has to be balanced against any future legal obligations imposed on the counsellor in various situations to make such records available for inspection by the client or some other authority.

The general rule of confidentiality does not apply where the safety of the client and/or others is at risk. This rule is a cause for concern regarding the issue of disclosure on the part of the counsellor. Where the safety of others is at risk, the ruling of Tarasoff vs. Regents of the University of California (1976) makes it clear that the counsellor has a "duty to warn" potential victims to protect them from harm. Also, where there is risk for the client, for example, a high risk of suicide, the counsellor ought to at least be able to consult with other professionals to develop a suitable plan of action. Junhke (1994) takes the position that in the case of a client's disclosure of suicidal thoughts, "consultation with an experienced supervisor or treatment team helps promote a multifaceted approach and decreases the probability of suicide resulting from a flawed treatment intervention" (p. 54). Gross & Robinson (1987) suggest that when the client indicates that there is clear and imminent danger to the client or others, the members must take reasonable personal action to inform responsible authorities. Consultation with other professionals should be used where possible (p. 340). Vandercreek and Knapp (1944) agree and point out that the rules of confidentiality hold that the privacy of the client is never absolute and must yield in certain situations such as when the physical safety of a human being is at stake (p. 51).

Informed Consent

Bray, Sheppard and Hays (1985), cited in Davis & Ritchie (1993), give three elements that determine adequate informed consent. The first deals with the clients capability to make reasonable decisions about engaging in counselling: First, can a client understand what is expected of him/her and what is expected of the counsellor? Second, there must be assurances that the client is entering the counselling process voluntarily. Third, the client must be able to understand what he/she is consenting to. In the latter, if the client is a minor, then, as Davis & Richie (1993) point out, informed consent must come from the parent or legal guardian. However, as Reamer (1991) points out, informed consent is now typically considered by the courts to be a process, and a signed form is only part of that process (p. 58).

It is a given that the information disclosed by the client is supposed to be treated in confidence. However, as Gross and Robinson (1987) point out, if the information poses a threat to self or others, the counsellor is required to make a judgment regarding the breaking of confidentiality and protecting other parties who might be in danger. This reflects the case of Tarasoff vs. Regents of the University of

California, where there is legal precedence for the "duty to warn" principal. Schwitzgeable & Schwitzgeabel (1980) cite the Supreme Court ruling in this case "that once a therapist does in fact determine, or under applicable professional standards reasonably should have determined, that a patient does pose serious danger of violence to others, he bears a duty to exercise reasonable care to protect the foreseeable victims of that danger" (p. 204).

The issue of violence in counselling is not confined only to the client committing a violent act. There is also the issue of violence by the counsellor against the client. Violence, such as sexual improprieties, assault and battery, although not common among counsellor-client interactions, does happen and counsellors ought to be informed of its occurrence and its consequences. Sexual relations with clients were not uncommon in the 60s and 70s and were held by some to not be violent, but were seen as therapeutic. However, both legal and ethical writings have indicated that such behavior can be harmful to clients. It is generally agreed by most helping professions today that sexual relations with clients in no way enhances their personal or social development. On the contrary, as Gross & Robinson (1987) point out, such relations tend to lessen their confidence and have negative social implications. Baylis (1993) concludes that therapist-patient sexual contact is unethical: it is a non-consensual activity that is inherently harmful. The Ontario Task Force on Sexual Abuse of Patients (cited in Baylis, 1993) states that there are no circumstances – none – in which sexual activity between a patient and a therapist is acceptable. Sexual activity between a patient and a therapist always represents sexual abuse, regardless of what rationalization or belief system the therapist chooses to use to excuse it. It is always the therapist's responsibility to know what is appropriate and never to cross the line into sexual activity.

Currently many counselling psychologists are faced with decisions regarding confidentiality and duty to warn when they are working with clients with HIV virus or the acquired immune deficiency syndrome (AIDS). Although confidentiality is an ethical principle integral to the codes of the helping professions, Stanard and Hazler (1995) point out it is not without limits. One of these limits is the "duty to warn" which results from the Tarasoff decision (1976). Stanard and Hazler (1995), citing Gehring (1982), note that the Tarasoff decision mandated three conditions sufficient to impose a "duty to warn": a) a special relationship, b) a reasonable prediction of conduct that constituted danger, and c) a foreseeable victim (p. 398). Kain (1988), cited in Stanard and Hazler (1995), states that an HIV-positive client engaging in high risk behavior with uninformed, identifiable partners does meet the three criteria for breaking confidentiality under Tarasoff (p. 398). However, Kain (1988), replying to Gray and Harding (1988, p. 224), notes that because sexual partners are in a position to refuse to engage in high risk sexual behavior then Tarasoff does not necessarily apply and that mandatory reporting in this case could produce more harm than good, and that reporting people with AIDS may indeed not be preventative, whereas education may be (p. 224). Herein lies a dilemma. Tarasoff may not automatically mandate warning, but rather as Lamb et al. (1989), cited in Stanard and Hazler (1995), point out, it mandates that the clinician exercise reasonable care. Kain (1988) appears to agree by implying that limiting confidentiality in the counselling process where AIDS is concerned can discourage disclosure and hence encourage the spread of the disease.

It appears that the counsellor's best recourse in handling complex ethical situations such as AIDS seems to lie in the study of ethical guidelines, reading the interpretations of others and then integrating that information into a personalized professional theory of counselling (Stanard & Hazler, 1995). Counselling psychologists who find themselves in ethical dilemmas when working with clients who are HIV positive or who have AIDS might choose to make use of Kitchener's (1985) five ethical principles: 1) respect autonomy, 2) do no harm, 3) benefit others, 4) be just and 5) be faithful. These principles are all inclusive and although collectively they do not provide answers, they do give a general bench mark or jumping off point for discussion and decision making.

There are few, if any, clearcut answers to the legal and ethical dilemmas a counselling psychologist may face in working with clients who are HIV positive or have AIDS (Lynch, 1993). However, Kitchener's (1985) ethical principles provide a framework for the mental health professional to use an appropriate decision-making model. However, as Lynch (1993) suggests, the reality is that each client's situation must be considered individually. The counselling psychologist must therefore use his/her best professional judgment. That judgment should be based on any number of professional decisions and writings. For example, professional judgments should include as a basis for decisions the principles of the Tarasoff decision (1976), Kitchener's (1985) five ethical principles, the Canadian Psychological Association and the Canadian Guidance and Counselling Association codes of ethics (1989) and the Canadian Code of Ethics for Psychologists (1988).

Tompkins and Melving (1993) suggest that possibly the most powerful protection available is afforded by operating within the professional/personal limitations of the practitioner. These limits include training, institutional policy, job description, professional code of ethics, and last but not least one's personal assessment of one's abilities. Tompkins and Melving (1993) also suggest that in most cases, counsellors who recognize these boundaries are adequately protected by liability insurance or stature. Adhering to the ethical standards, or professional interpretation of the standards, could be used as a defense. However, in situations where danger may or may not be present, taking no action would seem to be the most difficult decision to defend if someone is harmed (Davis & Ritchie, 1993, p. 27).

Reamer (1991) discusses several precautionary measures that professionals can take to balance their simultaneous obligation to protect the rights of clients who are HIV positive or have AIDS and who pose a genuine threat to third parties, while at the same time protect the clients' sexual partners from possible harm. These include practitioners becoming familiar with local laws and statutes that pertain to HIV and AIDS and any other sexually transmissible disease, consulting with local departments of health and justice to ascertain what the mandatory reporting procedures are in relation to HIV and AIDS, informing the clients of the limitations of confidentiality, and a knowledge of the standard guidelines regarding the practice of informed consent (p. 58).

Safety of Clients

Counsellors have a legal responsibility to provide a physically safe place for their counselling sessions. Legally, counsellors should be aware of their liability for negligence in this area. Cohen (1992) points out that counsellors should take all reasonable steps to ensure that the client suffers neither physical nor psychological harm during counselling. Cohen (1992) also points out that a counsellor cannot disclaim liability for negligence resulting in death or injury to the client. With this in mind he suggests that counsellors review periodically their need for professional indemnity insurance and take out such a policy when appropriate (p. 11).

Advice Giving

One only has to do a cursory look at the literature on counselling to come to the conclusion that counsellors generally do not see themselves as advice givers. On the contrary, counsellors are expected to help clients work through their problems, reach their own conclusions and do what is best for themselves. It is the counsellors prerogative to facilitate decision making and empower clients to take full responsibility for their own lives. However, as Cohen (1992) points out, in certain situations failure to give advice can be considered negligent just as much as giving bad advice (p. 15). As with many other legal and ethical issues advice giving in not a black and white issue but one that has a wide area of grey. All professions are required to exercise what has been broadly described as reasonable care and skill in the provision of their services to their clients. What is "reasonable" will be decided by the courts in cases of litigation. In deciding what is "reasonable," emphasis is placed on the standards of the profession gleaned from accepted writings and leading professional practitioners in the field (Cohen, 1992).

It is reasonable and indeed obligatory for the practicing counsellor to be up to date on theory and practical developments in the profession in order to ensure that the best service provided to clients is up to date and given within the parameters of reasonableness.

Counselling is a profession that deals with the total person. This implies that although there are rational discussions in the sessions, there is also in many therapy sessions a lot of emphasis on emotion. This inclusion of, and in many situations, emphasis on feelings and emotions, can effect predictability regarding outcomes in counselling. Counsellors, therefore, should be realistic in making predictions regarding the positive results of counselling (Cohen, 1992). They should approach counselling outcomes with openness and honesty. Given the volatility of the counselling process, counsellors ought to be cautious about entering into any kind of "iron clad" contract that would imply a "definite positive improvement" in the client's condition at the end of the counselling session(s). Setbacks in client behavior at certain points in the counselling process is not uncommon. If the client should terminate counselling during one of these setbacks and if a contract exists stating a guarantee of improvement, then the client could possibly sue the counsellor for breach of contract (Cohen, 1992).

Ethical Issues in Educational Settings

Bond (1992) suggests that in educational settings, two systems of ethical practices are generally used by counsellors. These are the integrated model, which emphasizes viewing the counsellor-institution relationship as the primary ethical perspective; and the differential model, which emphasizes the counsellor-client relationship as the starting point for an ethical understanding of the counsellor's role. These models suggest or at least imply that ethical practices, in a sense, depend on the particular ethical belief system of the institution in which counselling psychologists find themselves.

The integrated model is that which appears to be followed by most educational institutions. It complements the position of many school administrators that the counsellor is one of the staff and is first and foremost a "teacher." Not unlike other teachers, therefore, they have similar relationships and responsibilities to the institution. This model, on the surface, would seem to limit the function of the counsellor. However, this is not necessarily so, given the fact that the goals of the institution, namely, the effective education of the students, are the same for all staff regardless of title and/or the specific functions that they perform. However, on the other hand, there may be instances where the institution, in order to reach its goals, may impinge through its methods on the rights and/or dignity of the individual member. In such circumstances the counsellor may be obligated to adopt the differential model. This stance should not be interpreted by the institution as a lack of loyalty to the goals of the institution, but simply as an ethical issue which is resolvable within the guidelines of ethical behavior of the counsellor's professional code of ethics.

There appears to be a clear separation between the two models of ethical responsibility exposed by Bond (1992). However, it seems reasonable to assume that there should be room in institutions for a combination of both the integrated and the differential models. In some instances the differential model, which emphasizes the counsellor's commitment to the individual, would be the proper ethical mode to follow, whereas in other circumstances, the integrated model would be more ethical. The degree of tolerance for both will differ from institution to institution. The counsellor has the ethical responsibility to discuss these issues with the particular school administration before actually taking on the position of school counsellor.

These models of ethical behavior are very appropriate when one considers the changed and vastly heterogeneous composition of clients in the educational institution today. This range of individual differences in schools has been present historically. However, today, due in part to mainstreaming and/or integration, there are, besides the children who fit the so-called normal patterns of behavior, children who have learning disabilities, those who have criminal records, and those with moderate to severe behavioral problems. This vast difference in clients makes different demands on the work and consequent ethical and legal responsibilities of counsellors. Because of this heterogeneous arrangement of clients with whom the school counsellor has to work, it would appear to be unreasonable for the institution to insist on the adherence by the counsellor to either the integrated or the differential models. It is suggested therefore that there be open and frank discussion between the administrators and the counsellor as to when, and under what circumstances, the different models should be applied. For example, a student may come to the counsellor for help regarding their interpersonal relationships with a person of the opposite or same sex. Although this may be of monumental importance to the individual and indeed may be a major problem for him or her in terms of their progress in the school, it may not be an issue that the counsellor needs to take outside of the client-counsellor relationship. On the other hand, if the counsellor is informed by a client that he/she is doing something that will have some detrimental effect on the institution or specific members of the institution, then the counsellor may have to adopt the integrated model of ethics and involve other members of the institution.

In examining these models, one necessarily comes face to face with the issue of confidentiality in counselling. As Bond (1992) points out, the main difference in the integrated model and the differential model is the extent to which the counsellor in the institution involves others in the confidential relationship. The integrated model would necessarily involve in the counselling process significant others, both in the institution and in the life of the client. In this model, confidentiality is compromised based on the decision that the client's well being goes beyond and takes precedent over the counsellor/client relationship (Bond, 1992).

Counsellors who give strict adherence to the differential model would necessarily hold the position that whatever is said in the counselling relationship remains within the context of that setting. This puts the counsellor clearly on the horns of a dilemma. On the one hand, counsellors are committed to respect confidentiality, whereas on the other hand, there are circumstances where there may be a need, in order to help the client, or indeed for the safety of the client or of others, to involve significant others in the counselling process. In such circumstances it is best that the counsellor work through this dilemma with the client so that a compromise can be reached that will be of most benefit to the wellbeing of the client. In some cases, for example, where physical or emotional abuse is taking place or where the clients are a potential threat to themselves or others, it may not be a question of "if" the counsellor will involve others in the relationship but "when." We know, for example, that children who are being abused are very reluctant to reveal this information to anyone. However, if there is someone that they can relate to in "confidence," they are more apt to talk to them. It is a matter then for the counsellor to establish with such clients relationships that will enable them (the clients) to have the confidence to extend the discussion of their particular problem outside the specific relationship. This situation raises a number of questions: Can a counsellor reasonably and indeed ethically say that there is absolute strict adherence to confidentiality? At what point is the counsellor legally responsible for giving information gotten in the counselling relationship? Does the hiring institution have a right to "know" what the counsellor is doing and/or hearing in the counselling process? After all, the institution is paying the counsellor for the service. Do they have a right to know about the results of their investment? Where does the counsellors' responsibility to the client's request for confidentiality stop and when should it be shared with the institution? These are difficult and to some extent elusive questions. Denkowski & Denkowski (1982) point out that the professional requirement for safeguarding confidentiality is purely an ethical one. It is not therefore an illegal act for a counsellor to reveal in court what he/she heard in the confines of the counselling interview (p. 373). Counsellors, unlike barristers, do not have the protection of privileged communication with their clients. In fact, at writing, counsellors are required to answer questions put to them by a judge. Denkowski and Denkowski (1982) express the concern that, although counsellors are increasingly being mandated by law how they should execute this professional obligation of confidentiality, the extent of confidentiality that can be assured under these legal limitations is not absolute and is declining (p. 373).

Another ethical issue for counsellors working in educational settings is that of making sure they are not imposing their own particular values on to the client. It should be remembered that when working as a counsellor, particularly in an educational setting, the majority of clients will be "minors." These clients are particularly receptive to suggestions or messages given by adults, especially those adults whom they perceive to be in power positions. Counsellors should understand these relationships and be aware of their influence over their clients. They should be mindful that even though they may feel an ethical responsibility to their clients within the school system, they also have a legal responsibility to the parent of the child. Wagner (1981) suggests that the younger the client, the greater the counsellor's allegiance ought to be to the parent. Counsellors should be aware of the ease with which they can pass on their particular values to younger clients and should see it as their professional, as well as their ethical, responsibility not to in any way impose their own life values, and more specifically, their lifestyles, on these young clients. Imposing values or views on minors can result in legal action by the parents (Huey, 1986). Counsellors must challenge and assist students to explore their own and their parents values. They can then make their own decisions regarding lifestyle, etc., having given these due consideration.

Counselling in the Corporate World

Many private corporations provide counselling as one of their services offered to their employees. Ethical questions in these situations are on the one hand similar to those in the institutional setting, but on the other hand are somewhat different. The difference would appear to lie in the degree to which the aims of the organization differ. Whereas, for example, the goals of an educational institution are generally accepted as being for the betterment and advancement of the individual student, the goals of the firm are more likely to be more pointed towards the advancement of the firm. The question that could arise for the counsellor working in the firm is, who comes first, the firm or the individual? Sugarman (1992) asks, to what extent do the aims of an organization, over and above the aims of counselling, compromise counselling's ethical foundation? (p. 65) Does the counsellor help the worker adjust to the possible unhealthy working conditions in the work place or do they try to change the conditions? This, of course, is not dissimilar to what can happen in a school or university counselling situation. Many times counsellors have to decide if they should help the client adjust to the rules of the institution as opposed to working to change the rules to fit the needs of the client. When companies hire counsellors to work with their employees, they (the counsellors) are seen as part of the "team" and, not unlike the other members of the team, they have a responsibility to do all they can to ensure the efficiency and hence profitability of the organization. The rationale behind this belief is that what is good for the organization will ultimately be good for the employee. Sadly, this does not always work out in that way. Therefore, there has to be some middle ground whereby both the employee and the company will benefit from the counselling program. Counsellors have to be aware of the point where counselling benefits the organization at the individual's expense. As Sugarman

(1992) points out, the opposite of who benefits from counselling at work is, who is or might be harmed by it?

Counsellors working in the marketplace also can experience similar difficulties regarding the issue of confidentiality as when working in institutions. When counselling is sought through self-referral, this may not be a problem. However, when employees are referred for counselling by the employer, there could be problems in this area. When counselling is required by the employer, counsellors have to be aware of such questions as, will the company insist on information regarding the client's discussions and progress? The information or lack of it that the counsellor gives may very well become an ethical issue (Sugarman, 1992).

Dual Relationships in Counselling

Among the many ethical issues that confront counselling psychologists is that of dual relationships. Herlihy & Corey (1992) describe dual relationships as two different relationships operating either concurrently or consecutively. These relationships may both be professional, or a combination of professional and personal. An example of the former is a counsellor who is also a teacher, while an example of the latter is a counsellor who is a client's friend or lover. Counsellors should understand the elements and ramifications of dual relationships, because they have serious and usually harmful effects upon the professional counsellor-client relationship.

There are clear guidelines that govern the counsellor-client relationship. Of primary importance are the guidelines against dual relationships. The Canadian Guidance & Counselling Association, in An Ethical Standards Casebook (1988), states that the counsellor should respect the client and shield them from any therapy-related problems. A member's primary obligation is to respect the integrity and promote the welfare of the counselee(s) whether the counselee(s) is (are) assisted individually or in groups. In a group setting, the member-leader is also responsible for protecting the individuals from physical and/or psychological trauma resulting from interaction within the group (p. 24).

This guideline is further elaborated upon through various case studies and hypothetical scenarios. In one of the scenarios, the client suggests to the counsellor that they begin dating. The counsellor declines because such behavior is inappropriate for a professional counsellor-client relationship (p. 26). If the counsellor accepted the invitation, they would enter into the dual relationship of both counsellor and friend/lover. The American Association for Counselling and Development (AACD) is very clear in its guidelines in discouraging dual relationships. Dual relationships with clients that might impair the member's objectivity and professional judgment (e.g., as with close friends or relatives) must be avoided and/or the counselling relationship terminated through referral to another competent professional (cited in Herlihy & Corey, 1992).

Herlihi & Corey (1992) suggest that although the language differs in its clarity, clearly the counselling profession frowns on dual relationships because of the complications and problems that may arise. Herlihy & Corey (1992) suggest a number of reasons why dual relationships can create problems: they are pervasive and occasionally unavoidable, difficult to recognize, there is differing advice from experts concerning dual relationships, and they may be harmful, but not always (p. 7).

Dual relationships are by the very nature of the work place inevitable. Herlihy & Corey (1992) give the example of a counsellor who works in the counselling centre of a university and, in addition to these duties, teaches some courses. It is very possible that the counsellor will have, among their students, one or more clients. Such dual relationships are unavoidable. Dual relationships are often as difficult to recognize as they are pervasive. A counsellor could be in a dual relationship without even knowing it. Most likely, this would arise when the relationship occurs consecutively (Herlihy & Corey, 1992, p. 8). Some would say that as long as the two relationships are not concurrent, then there should not be a problem. But this is not always the case. As Pope & Vasquez (1991) point out, "the mere fact that the two roles are apparently sequential rather than clearly concurrent does not, in and of itself, mean that the two relationships do not constitute a dual relationship" (p. 112).

There is much disagreement among experts regarding dual relationships. Some suggest that the ethical concerns are guidelines only, and not rigid, uncompromising rules (Herlihy & Corey, 1992). Ultimately, suggest some counsellors, issues such as dual relationships are matters for the judgment of the persons involved. On the other hand, there are those who argue in favor of strict adherence to guidelines, thereby avoiding any ambiguous situations.

In the counselling relationship there are certain expectations on the part of both the client and the counsellor. Where a dual relationship exists, there could easily arise a conflict in expectation; in other words there could be some covert or unexpressed expectation on the part of either. Herlihy & Corey (1992) give the following example: Jim is giving Mary counselling, but there is also a friendship between the two. During one of their sessions Jim points out a problem area in Mary's personality and she is very hurt by the remark. Jim is acting in his role as a counsellor, yet Mary is interpreting his comments in the context of friendship. Immediately a problem arises, because the expectations of both people in the dual relationship are different. If counsellor and client share an intimate and sexual relationship in addition to a professional one, then the problems are even greater. Clients may feel guilty, sexually confused, unsure of their role in the professional relationship, angry, even suicidal, when sex is a factor in the relationship (p. 23-25).

Herlihy & Corey (1992) point out that dual relationships can produce divided loyalties and a loss of objectivity. In the above example, what would happen if Jim does not tell Mary about her problem because he is afraid of hurting her? As a professional counsellor, Jim has an obligation to counsel Mary; but if he does not because of personal concerns, he is not being objective and impartial. Jim's loyalties are torn between professional obligations and personal interests. Unfortunately, in this case, both Jim and Mary are victims because Mary does not receive the help she deserves and Jim is, in this instance, a failure as an objective professional (p. 12).

Dual relationships can create problems with regard to power and influence. Herlihy & Corey (1992) give the following example: suppose a client asks the counsellor for a recommendation for a very responsible job? The counsellor knows the client's history, but accepts anyway. If the counsellor says anything in the recommendation that would cause the employer to reconsider, the client's chance of obtaining employment is in jeopardy. Counsellors should realize that they hold much power and influence over a client (p. 13).

However, there are some possible benefits of dual relationships. Not all dual relationships are harmful. In fact, these relationships range from harmful to beneficial. For example, the mentor relationship between teacher and student is an instance of a dual role that is crucial. A good teacher of counselling will not only teach but will challenge students to evaluate their values so that education becomes a vehicle of personal growth rather than just imparting information that has little effect (Herlihy & Corey, 1992, p. 16).

The issue of dual relationships is of importance to the counselling profession because of the potential impact it can have on the counsellor-client relationship. The role of a counsellor is to help, in whatever professional way possible, a client to continue the art of personal growth. Therefore, counsellors must be vigilant of any and all problems that could arise. In the case of the inevitable dual relationship, counsellors should understand how they develop, their ramifications and the proper way to handle them. There are various opinions on the role of these relationships and counsellor's duties in light of them.

Dual relationships, like every ethical issue, are very difficult, if not impossible to resolve. The only hope is to continue to approach the problem in an authentic way. That way involves being attentive to the dynamics that operate in any given counselling relationship, respond to them in an intelligent and reasonable way, and act responsibly by keeping the interests of the client uppermost in mind.

The above discussion merely scratches the surface of this ever-growing issue for counsellors. I have tried to highlight some of the legal and ethical concerns that counsellors face in their day-to-day practice. Ethical and legal issues, although on the surface they appear to be straightforward, are indeed complicated and subject to many different interpretations. Within each there are many questionable situations in which counsellors may find themselves. These depend on many factors including social customs and expectations, situation and conditions of employment, client demands and expectations. As professionals working in the helping professions, counselling psychologists are expected to be able to recognize and understand ethical and legal issues as they arise. More importantly, they ought to know what steps to take to deal with them effectively. As Gross & Robinson (1987) point out, the task is not an easy one. Only through continuing education, knowledge of the law, knowledge of ethical standards, consultation with peers and supervisors, and knowledge and understanding of self will effective solutions be realized. These solutions are the only avenues that lead directly to the ultimate goal of the profession, namely, the continued enhancement of client welfare.

Chapter 9
The Counsellor as a Reflective Practitioner*

In recent years the concept of reflective practice has come to the forefront in much of the literature regarding professional development. This movement has been particularly strong in relation to teacher education. The assumption underlying this movement is that teachers, if given the opportunity, can be taught to reflect on their own experiences, in their own experiences, or both on and in their experiences. This reflective practice will positively enhance their own and their students' personal and professional growth and practice (Osterman, 1990; Argyris and Schon, 1974). When reading this literature, I was challenged to ask: What are the implications, if any, for this concept of reflective practice in counsellor education?

It appears that the basis of counselling theory is rooted in a reflective/analytical/experiential process. Implicit in the belief of most counselling theorists is the opinion that counsellors should encourage the client to reflect on his/her particular situation and experiences so as to be empowered to act. Counselling is seen as not doing for or doing to, but as a vehicle for the release of potential (Frankl, 1955; Ellis, 1962; Rogers, 1951). This process appears to be germane to the very essence of counselling. In some sense there is a concern with what we do in counselling as much as what we think about counselling. The question is whether counsellor or teacher interns are asked to conform to what is, or to challenge, through critical and reflective thought, the status quo. Is it the goal of counselling/teaching that a person seek out fulfillment, driven by social righteousness, or effect social change driven by critical reflection? This dilemma occupies much of the thinking in the education of professionals in institutions today. There is, for example, the belief that the goals of educational institutions are not necessarily in agreement with those of the hiring agencies. Thus, the concept of reflective practice is often perceived as a waste of time or a frill indulged in by those who do not have to hire.

In our research with teacher interns (Doyle et al., 1994), we decided to work with them in light of what they think about teaching as much as what they do in teaching. This process is a foundation principle of the Schon (1983) thesis underlying the role of the reflective practitioner. Through this reflective process we tried to establish a link between theory and practice that is not only transformative personally

---

*A version of this chapter was originally published in Doyle et al.

for the intern, but also for the students with whom they are and will be working. In a way, we tried to empower our interns by acknowledging their voices and stories as valid for their own professionalism. However, we also are cognizant of the transfer of this empowerment to the students and co-teachers with whom they work. It is a process of giving voice to interns who, in turn, will acknowledge the voice of all those with whom they meet in their profession.

This chapter will review some of the theoretical underpinnings of the concept of reflective teaching. It will attempt to relate the process of reflection to the practice of counselling and look at counselling literature to ascertain if there is a link between the two.

Teaching, like other professions, is affected by quick fixes or fads. When the notion of Reflective Teaching was introduced, it was seen as no exception. However, during the past ten years or so there has been a surge of literature which has changed that opinion. It has now become an accepted way of thinking and practicing in teacher education. Possibly the most influential writer in the field of reflective practice, though not an educator in the strict sense of the term, was Schon (1983). Schon gave the process of reflection the impetus it needed, and hence it has become a professionally sound and integral part of many teacher education programs. Feiman-Nemser (1990) makes this point clearly when he states one can hardly pick up a professional journal or attend a professional meeting without encountering the terms reflective teaching and teacher education. Fifteen years ago the same would have been true of the terms competency-based and performance-based teacher education. These conceptual alternatives reflect different views of teaching and learning to teach and suggest different orientations to the preparation of teachers (p. 212). This comment makes sense when we give but a cursory glance at the literature, and one can instantly come up with a list of writers researching and writing about this topic (Gore & Zeichner, 1991; Clift, Houston and Pugach, 1990; Calderhead, 1989; Ross, 1989; Smyth, 1987; Cruickshank, 1985; Cruickshank and Applegate, 1981).

Reflective teaching is not a new idea. Socrates emphasized inquiry and reflective practice in his teaching. Piaget believed that learning depends on integrating experience with reflection. John Dewey was obviously thinking along these lines, since his philosophy of education emphasizes student-centredness, individualization of learning and the empowerment of the learner to take hold of his or her process of learning (Zeichner & Gore, 1990). Embodied in this philosophy of reflective teaching is the concept that people hold the potential to think about and act on their own thoughts and actions. According to the Dewey philosophy, restrictions on or disempowerment of the individual's freedom to learn as an individual would necessarily restrict the act of true, as opposed to institutionally sanctioned, reflection. Houston et al. (1990) state that, to reflect, an individual must not only be free to think but also feel empowered to think. When clients are permitted to give credence to their own voice, we also give them a sense of belief in the power of their thoughts. Greene (1986) states that empowerment involves the person inspiring hitherto unknown voices to rediscover personal memories and articulate them in the presence of others whose space they can share. This demands the capacity to unveil and disclose.

Some general attempts have been made to put degrees of reflective practices on a scale (Gore & Zeichner, 1991; Van Manen, 1977; Simmons et al., 1989). They generally fall into four steps:

1. reflection on what is taught;
2. reflection on strategies of teaching or pedagogical intervention;
3. reflection on the social/cultural milieu of schooling in general and more specifically classroom dynamics; and
4. reflection on the needs, interests and developmental maturity of clients.

These steps raise the question of what level or levels of reflection the counsellor or teacher needs to practice. More to the point, a counsellor or teacher might want to think about reflection within the variety of presenting problems and situations in which their clients/students find themselves.

Reflective practice by its very nature is not a technique or tool to be pulled out when the situation demands it. Indeed, it has to be accepted into one's professional repertoire as a natural way of thinking. It has to become the "sine qua non" of one's professionalism. Socrates was revered, not for his knowledge so much as for his ability to help students know themselves and analyze the learning situation and then to challenge his students to analyze and reflect and arrive at their own solutions or at least alternative ways of seeing the problem. John, one of the interns with whom we worked, captured this thought when he said:

> but there will come a time when you won't have other people around and you have to make decisions for yourself... get your views in and see how far they go and what reaction you get to them...

This is no doubt a common understanding of the practice of the 90s counsellor for the 21st century. In post modern society, with a strong emphasis on counselling as a shared process and the clients' stories (narratives) as central to the action (White & Epston, 1990), counsellors are not necessarily appreciated solely for their knowledge as much as for their ability to bring clients to an understanding of their particular problems. To have this ability, the counsellor must be able to reflect in action: think divergently and critically and recognize shades of distinction within problems (Schon, 1983). It is this sense of reflection that enables the counsellor to look beyond professional knowledge and training, that is, the content to which he or she has been exposed. Through this process of questioning, challenging and reflecting, counsellors are given permission to question the technical, rational approach to professionalism and to bring to their professional lives their own thoughts and feelings and actions, which will enhance their understanding and their knowledge. Reflective practice can not only help in counselling, but it can enable us to learn to communicate with others as a way of making sense of what we are doing.

In a sense, reflective practice offers the opportunity to counsellors to see their profession from a metacognitive and metaphysical dimension. It requires thinking about their thoughts on their professional activity and development (Kimmins, 1985). Roger (1951) alludes to this when he talks about listening with understanding or active listening (p. 331). Schon (1983) makes a similar point. When a practitioner makes sense of a situation he perceives to be unique, he sees it as something actually present in his repertoire: To see "this" site as "that," one is not to subsume the first under a familiar category or rule. It is rather to see the unfamiliar unique situation as both similar to and different from the familiar one; without at first to say similar or different with respect to what (p. 62). This is, in a sense, a reflection on one's own reflection in action. It is the kind of meta-thinking which Kimmins (1985) talks about and is the crux or quintessence of the process of reflective practice.

It is important to note that reflection in the Schon sense is not totally an individual process, "it is not a process devoid of social interaction" (Schon, 1983). To some degree, then, it is a product, enhanced and cultivated by the two-way semi-permeable sac which separates persons. That is to say, the individual doing the reflection is influenced by the social web and networking of systems in which he/she lives. At the same time, the person's social milieu is influenced by his/her reflection on it. This is to say that the person not only sees what the social context demands (technical rationality) but changes or adds to it by his/her own thinking about it. Each person in a sense brings something, their own experience, etc., to a situation which contributes to the reflective process.

This process of bringing one's own voice to the particular context is what Schon (1983) speaks of when he discusses professionals being out of step with changing situations and practices. Existing bodies of knowledge or ways of acquiring such knowledge are unable to handle the complexity, uncertainty, instability, uniqueness and value conflicts which are increasingly perceived as central to the world of professional practice (p. 14). This idea is apropos to counselling. The social context in which counselling takes place today is complex and diverse. It is not sufficient for the counsellor to "learn" all that is to be known about current counselling theory or all the angles of therapeutic intervention or indeed to be familiar with research that, for the most part, is dated when published. It seems reasonable to expect the counsellor, who works in a milieu that is ever-changing and complex, to be capable of and to have the professional competency to exercise the process of reflection on and in action within that socio-cultural cosmos. Counsellors ought to have a sense of the sometimes multiple impingements which come to bear on a client's life. They must not only be able to draw on knowledge as learned from texts, they must, while in action, be able to analyze the assumptions of their knowledge base and indeed generate their own knowledge base given the general framework of their cultural, social, economic and educational milieu. This analysis of basic assumptions and development of new knowledge will enhance in counsellors a more critical and positive look at the presented problem and thus facilitate the process of helping. It will, in the Rogerian (1961) sense, have the effect of allowing the counsellor and the client to be free from the shackles of what was and what will be and, given the realities, open the way for the search for solutions in a 'what could be' sense. Counsellors are thus empowered to be truly professional, and clients are empowered to be an integral part of the solution.

This interplay of knowledge development and reflective analysis is important for the education of future counsellors. They should be able not only to practice skills and learn theory, but also be cognizant of the need to critically reflect on the practice and application of these skills and theories. There should be ample time in their education to analyze, redefine, and re-evaluate the various skills and theories put forth and not to accept them as meta-narratives and carved in stone. This point I believe could be added to the necessary conditions for counselling as laid out by Rogers (1961).

In professions such as counselling, teaching and medicine, there has always been and still is the controversy of integrating existing theory and practice into present day context. It is in the interest of counselling, with its strong social/cultural underpinnings, that its professionals be able not only to acquire and use existing knowledge, but also be capable of generating new knowledge. If this new knowledge is arrived at through reflection in/on action, then it should encompass in its structure both the theory and practice of the past and present and bridge the gap that gives rise to relevant and newer ways of thinking and acting in present context.

If we are to assume that part of being a professional counsellor is to be able to bring about new knowledge from already existing knowledge and practice, then we must assume that the counsellor does possess a practical theory. This assumes a sagacious life incorporating a person's private, integrated – but ever-changing – system of knowledge, experience and values relevant to teaching practice or counselling practice at any time. It differs from craft knowledge or receipt knowledge, which often assumes knowledge to be static. It is bringing to bear on situations one's total life experiences. It is, in a sense, a meta-cognitive process superimposed on the totality of one's integrated life experiences (Handal & Lauvas, 1987).

The bringing together of the totality of one's experience or practical theory helps enhance the necessary condition of empathy (Rogers, 1961). This relationship or oneness with another's mind/self is greatly facilitated by the presence of one's practical theory. We constantly live in conflict of the two worlds of being and becoming. Through the art of empathy we can look at the world of being and see where the client is in her/his here-and-now existence. True empathetic understanding necessarily includes our ability to see our world and that of our clients where we and they are in the here and now. Empathy is more than a simple scan of the person's inner thoughts. It is an in-depth understanding of the values and ideals, feelings and experiences of the person. This like-minded responsiveness can empower the client to participate in the therapy process as active learners. This enables clients to develop and reflect on their own practical theory, thus empowering them to become reflective practitioners in their own right.

The challenge to the counsellor is to help the client move from a static place or status quo in his/her life, that is from a place of "stuckness," to a place more in tune with what could be, or to move from the specific context of self to a world which has greater interpersonal scope and to a place where he/she is free from accepting predetermined outcomes. The existentialists May, Angel & Ellenberger (1958) bring out this point in defining the relationship of self to include self and the world. The idea is also linked to the third level of the three levels of reflection which Van Manen (1977) outlines with the following scale of reflection: (1) the reflection of rationality, concerning the acceptance of and reflection on the status quo; (2) practical reflectivity, in a recognition that action is somehow related to an outcome or value; and (3) reflection that is critical and analytical, with concern for the outcomes as it relates to broader, more global moral/ethical issues. In a sense the client weighs outcomes in terms not only of self-development but with broader understanding and concern for such things as justice or moral right and self in relation to others.

Rogers' (1961) and others' humanistic approaches to counselling talk about the phenomenological world of the client. This essentially says that each person has a private world (practical theory) of experience of which he/she is the centre. The counsellor can help clients restructure and/or reframe through reflection a personal theory in light of his/her cultural milieu. In Rogerian terms, the main aim in therapy is to help the individual client, in the safety of the therapeutic relationship, to experience to the limit of what he/she is. "They can be and are experienced in a fashion that I like to think of as a 'pure culture' so that the person is his fear or he is his anger or he is his tenderness, or whatever" (p. 111-112).

It is in this pure culture that "I," the counsellor, can help clients find personal growth through reflection on their personal theories and private worlds. The reconstruction of assumptions and personal beliefs through reflection will enable the counsellor to be critically reflective and thus allow clients to challenge in a constructive way their beliefs and feelings about themselves. Otherwise these get in the way of the therapeutic process. It is interesting to note here what Kierkegaard, the Danish philosopher, said about the exigency of finding and knowing the real self without the trappings and assumed cultural indicated thoughts. Rogers (1961), taking a passage from Kierkegaard, points out that the most common despair is "to be in despair of not choosing, or willing, to be oneself; but the deepest form of despair is to choose to be another than himself. On the other hand, to will to be that self which one truly is, is indeed the opposite of despair" (p. 110).

It is in the critical reflective process that we can challenge many of the assumptions we have about ourselves, thus freeing ourselves of these many-faceted, culturally-induced belief systems or misconceptions. Thus we are enabled to enhance our commitment to change, growth and the acceptance of self as changed.

The counsellor as reflective practitioner, like the concept of reflection itself, is not new. When one reads the established theories of counselling, one sees throughout a distinct strain of reflection in and on action (Rogers, 1961; Perls, 1969; Frankl, 1963; Ellis, 1962). In these theories, there is the recognition of the individual's need to reflect on his/her total experiences and to have the freedom to choose values and goals and pursue his/her own lifestyle in a manner that is congruent with the outcomes of this reflection.

The existentialists May and Sartre no doubt relate well to the thought embodied in the meaning of reflection since existentialism is concerned with the individual importance within self. Existentialism recognizes, as does the process of reflection, that every person has a unique experience (personal theory). People can react and add to their situations by recognizing the value of another individual's formal theory. We exist in a world of reality and we bring our own personal meaning to that reality. The recognition by the reflective practitioner of this basic inner quality that I posit begs an existentialist view of our world in the therapeutic process.

Indeed, conflict often arises in the counselling process between the goals of self and those of the greater group. Reflection in and on action implies that the practitioner becomes aware of three things: (1) what effect the action or thought has on self and self-growth; (2) its impact on the profession; and (3) its impact on those with whom the counsellor is working or living. Reflection on action in counselling similarly impacts on the practitioner and the client, which impacts on those within the social milieu of both.

In the affective approach to counselling, Rogers (1951) speaks of the phenomenal field of the individual, his/her private world and the sum of his/her experiences. In therapy the counsellor has to be aware that the client is reacting to personal perceived experiences and not necessarily to a reality as perceived by others. This perceptual field, internal frame of reference, or, as called in the reflective theory, practical theory, greatly affects individual's interaction with his/her present reality. In a similar way, Ellis (1962) speaks of the ABC approach to counselling. He contends that it is not A – the behavior – that is the real problem, nor is it C – the outcome of our behavior; instead, it is B – our perception of the outcome – that creates our anxiety. What we bring to the outcome, that is, the totality of our experience, influences how we react/feel about a given action. These theories do emphasize the importance of the practical theory of the individual in assessing, understanding and giving meaning to situations or new experiences. This emphasis is in line with the statement by Schon (1983) that when a practitioner makes sense of a situation he perceives to be unique, he sees it as something actually present in his repertoire. In other words, it is or becomes part of the perceptual field of that person. Kimmis (1985) refers to this as a dialectical process in that the thinking of the individual is shaped by a cultural/social context and that the social and cultural context is itself shaped by the thought and action of individuals. As counsellors and clients pursue their goals, they must be able to find ways of helping each other reflect on this process, and in the existential sense find their own existence within it. This, in the Rogerian sense, is part of the process of self-actualizing. Hultgren (1987), similar to Rogers, talks about reflection, and sees the process from a phenomenological perspective. She stresses the idea of reconstruction of the self as teacher. In this sense to be reflective is to do an intrapersonal search in order to give meaning to the process of teaching and the person's place in that process. Reflection then can redesign and shape one's feelings and knowledge about counselling and about the client as part of that process. Through reflection, the client and the counsellor can redirect energy and redefine their thinking about behavior or problems. Reflection affects counsellors insofar as it entices them to construct and reconstruct their ideas of the self as counsellor and the self as caring professional.

It is evident that the role of the counsellor was never that of assuming the curing or healing role. Rather, the role has been to empower the client to take control of his/her development as a person. In this empowering process, the recognition of the client's and counsellor's development of practical theory is essential. Reflection here plays a key role in helping both the client and the counsellor come to an understanding of the ability of the client to come to grips with how he/she sees his/her own thought processes and behaviors. In reflecting on and thus learning about these processes, the client would be encouraged to take self-initiatives and become responsible, that is, self-directing his/her life. The question is: Who owns the problem? The process of counselling is aimed at empowerment of clients and having them become self-directed in their developmental process. This self-direction is meant to be holistic in the sense that the client, with the assistance of the counsellor, ought to be able to plan, execute, reflect on and evaluate his/her own behavior from personal experience. This process is closely linked to what Rogers (1961) describes as the continually changing world of experience in which the client exists. This private world, which constitutes the practical theory of the individual, is not always in the awareness of the individual, but needs to be brought to consciousness. It is through the process of reflection that the person can react to his/her private world, not as the counsellor sees it, but as the client perceives it. This, of course, implies that the reality for the client as he/she perceives it is not necessarily similar to that which the counsellor sees or perceives. It is the recognition of this fact by the counsellor or any other helping professional that will help facilitate growth in self-awareness and also professional growth and development. This recognition of the understanding of the inner, private world of the individual requires what I have referred to earlier as empathy, that is, the ability to understand the person's internal frame of reference or private world or practical theory. Coupled with this understanding must be the ability to let the person know that you do understand this world and that this world is an OK place to be. Truax and Mitchell (1971) have described this ability to identify with the client's world as similar to the relationship we build with the main character of a novel:

> *The state that as we come to know some of his wants, some of his needs, some of his achievements and some of his followers, and some of his values, we find ourselves living with the other person much as we do the hero or heroine of a novel. We come to know the person from his own internal viewpoint and thus gain some understanding and flavor of his moment-by-moment experience.*

Empathy described in this way shows how we, by letting the other person speak to us from his/her own personal frame of reference, can allow that person to show us his/her personal world in his/her terms, rather than ours. This freedom enhances learning in both parties and implies listening without making judgments as to the rightness or wrongness of the person's experiences. By establishing this non-evaluative climate, clients can be free to become more understanding of themselves and consequently of others. Rogers (1961) describes this process in this way: If I am truly open to the way life is experienced by another person. If I can take his world into mine – then I run the risk of seeing life in his way, of being changed myself, and we all resist change, so we tend to view this other person's word only in our terms, not in his. We analyze and evaluate it, we do not understand it. But when someone understands how it feels and seems to be me without waiting to analyze or judge me, then I can blossom and grow in that climate (p. 90).

This empathetic process is closely related to the third level of reflection explained by Van Manen (1977). The counsellor is in a position where he/she is unable to be removed from the realities in which the client lives or perceives he/she lives. The act of counselling cannot take place without co-existing within the aspirations, hopes and difficulties which form part of the culture of the client. Certainly we must have the client describe the problem, but we have to get at the meaning behind these descriptors. In a way the evaluation that I put on the description is not necessarily the real truth behind these descriptors. It is rather the client's experience that is the better informed. It is his/her personal, practical theory that gives real meaning to his/her discourse. If we can provide a kind of empathetic relationship, then the person will discover within himself/herself the capacity, based on his/her own experiences, to use the counselling time for growth, change and personal/professional growth.

The counsellor as a reflective practitioner is not using a new concept, but neither is reflection simply a new handle on an old pan. The act of reflection has always been part of counselling; but in the past, reflection was focused on the client. The change in focus to include the counsellor puts a new spin on the process. Counsellors need to go beyond simply encouraging or suggesting that the client be reflective, the counsellor must also become a reflective practitioner. This can be done conjointly with the client in counselling, or during post sessional discussions with other co-professionals. If counsellors are to facilitate change, they must adopt a theory of action which enhances human activity, responsibility, self-actualization, learning and effectiveness (Argyres & Schon, 1974).

The application of reflective action theory will inhibit counsellors from simply following their own thoughts and feelings in a robotic fashion, and help them question and/or explore the undercurrents which drive them. Clients do not usually enter counselling with a disposition to reconstruct their existence or behavior and thereby impact positively on society. They come because they want to fit in as they are or to ask society to fit their agenda. They want to be fixed so that they can be happy. The assumption is that a purely technical, rational, efficiency process in counselling, without due consideration of the broader notion of personal-social development, will secure peace and social acceptance. Zeichner and Gore (1990) in summarizing Van Manen's domains of reflection, refer to cultural reflection. This term goes beyond merely technical/rational reflection and includes the moral and ethical criteria in discovering practical plans of action. In a sense then, it is a question of whether our actions fit our agenda for happiness, but also whether our reflection on our experiences, activities and goals leads toward a life that is characterized by justice, caring, and compassion. If positive growth is to take place in clients' attitudes and behavior, then counsellors must personally be involved in and empower clients to be active participants in a reflective process. The best vantage point for understanding behavior of an individual is from the internal frame of reference of the person and how some of this inner self becomes externalized. The "self" is best structured and developed through interactions with the environment, with self and with others (Rogers, 1961).

Chapter 10
Counselling in Schools:
Counsellor/Teacher/Administrator Relationships

The practice of counselling psychology permeates most of the various work places in our post modern society. It is an important part of programming in schools, hospitals and corporate organizations. Counselling in institutional settings brings with it a unique brand of issues and problems, not the least of which is the relationship of the counsellor with administrators and other staff members. This chapter will look at one institutional work place, namely, the school. There are many different issues that arise in counselling psychology within the school situation. In keeping with the holistic and systemic approach to counselling in this text, I have selected two issues that I feel impact most directly on the role of the school counsellor, namely, the role of teachers and administrators in the counselling process.

Counsellor/Teacher Relationships

When school counselling was first introduced as an integral part of the educational service offered to students, counsellors worked for the most part as isolated professionals, who separated themselves almost completely from the everyday operations of the school. Counsellors looked after the students' psycho/social needs, while teachers concerned themselves with educational needs. There was little interaction between these two groups of professionals. With the growth and application of more holistic and less atomized approaches to dealing with people and their problems, counsellors and educators in the school began to see the problems inherent in this kind of professional isolation. The application of systems theory to the social sciences (Bertalanffy, 1968) as a method of working with and seeking solutions to human behavior problems has been a major factor in bringing about this change in thinking. Systems theory, with its emphasis on interactive counselling, advocates that it is paradoxical on the one hand for counsellors to purport to effectively help students function as a whole persons, while at the same time operate in a system that divides them into separate atomistic parts. Counsellors and others who work in the helping professions need to understand that although a counsellor may spend hours counselling a client in an attempt to change his or her behavior, those hours are of little value if the environment outside the counselling office does not support or indeed is not aware of the problems of the client. Both counsellors and teachers need to realize that a student's problem is neither developed or resolved in isolation. Rather, problems exist within a set of systems and sub-systems in which all those involved in the life of the client play an important role. In school counselling, it is paramount that teachers play a vital and active role in helping solve student problems. Teachers are indeed an integral part of the solution. It is clear that a good relationship between counsellor and teacher is an essential part of an effective counselling practice.

For a systemic approach towards solving student problems to work effectively, a cooperative and open relationship between teachers and counsellors is essential. However, good relationships between counsellors and teachers are often hampered by misconceptions or misunderstandings which teachers have about the counsellor and the counselling process. In some instances, teachers find it difficult to accept the counsellor as a "specialist in human relations" in their school. They feel this way because to admit the need for such "specialists" implies that somehow they (the teachers) are wanting or limited in their ability to understand their students (Kushel, 1967). In other circumstances, teachers believe the counsellor is on staff to solve all the problems of the student body that others were not able to solve. They use the office as a drop-off point for students whom they feel they cannot handle or, in some cases, with whom they do not want to work. Sometimes when counsellors become part of the school staff, teachers adopt the attitude that behavior problem students are no longer their responsibility. Instead they expect the counsellor to "fix the problem." These expectations of the counsellor by teachers show a lack of understanding of the role of the counsellor in the school (Avis, 1982).

Other problems in counsellor/teacher relationships arise when teachers misunderstand the specifics involved in the process of counselling. Some teachers, for instance, do not recognize counselling as a lengthy and difficult process which requires time and consultation in order to arrive at sometimes minuscule positive results. Other teachers may get caught in the numbers game and resent that the number of students they have to contend with on a daily basis is monumental compared with the small number of students seen by the counsellor. A further misconception is that teachers may sometimes see the office space provided to the counsellor as out of proportion with their own individual working space, which usually consists of a "cubby hole" in the corner of the staff lounge.

Teacher misunderstanding of the counsellors role can also occur when counsellors are seen as being excused from certain extra curricular duties within the school. Teachers are often asked, in the course of their everyday work, to teach, to enforce school policy, to carry out various supervisory duties, to monitor tardiness, to take care of truancy concerns, to police the restrooms, to function as substitute teachers, to sit in study halls for students on detention, and to serve as supervisors at school events (Herlihy & Corey, 1992). However, counsellors have to be excused from many of these duties since they are often in conflict with the primary role of counsellor. The dual roles of disciplinarian/informant and counsellor may easily create a conflict of interest for the counsellor. A reputation as a person who "asks you to trust them at one time, and turns you in at another time" could keep many prospective clients away from the counsellor (Herlihy & Corey, 1992). Teachers who have a misconception of the counselling process may fail to understand this part of the counsellor's role and take the view that counsellors are simply not carrying their share of the extra-curricular load. In such situations, the counsellor should take the initiative to communicate with teachers and try to create an understanding of the reason behind this different expectation of the role of a counsellor. Creating this understanding of the role of the counsellor is ultimately the responsibility of the individual counsellor. In many instances, counsellors themselves have contributed to the misconceptions of their role. They have exacerbated these misunderstandings by maintaining an isolationist work policy towards teachers and other professionals.

Given the present generalist nature of most counsellor education programs, and the complexity of dealing with the human condition, counsellors need to recognize their professional limitations. These constraints, coupled with time limitations, makes it impossible for counsellors to work effectively with all cases which are referred to them. It is important, therefore, that counsellors and the teachers be able to decide on a general policy regarding referral. This policy should specify if and when clients ought to be referred to other specialists counsellors, and/or to a professional other than a counsellor. When dealing with referrals, it is essential that reasons for referral be clearly understood by both the teacher and counsellor, and that the lines of communication between referring professionals remain clear and open.

When counsellors become completely overloaded with work, failure to say no to requests for help by teachers and/or students, or failure to refer, can result in incomplete work. This can lead to the perception that the counsellor is unprofessional. Also, counsellors must accept that in some instances they are unable to help clients and these cases are better dealt with by referral to other more appropriate professionals. Counsellors must not assume sole responsibility for all the problems of the student body and more importantly, give the impression that they can solve them. To do so is to set the stage for professional catastrophe and ultimate failure.

Relationships between teachers and counsellors can be enhanced and much of the above conflict avoided if both sides become more aware of each other's role in the educative process of the students within the school. A better understanding of their reciprocal roles would help both counsellors and teachers to realize that their specific roles actually complement and don't conflict with each other. Teaching and counselling have similar goals and definitions. Both the school counsellor and the teacher are involved in "educational" processes, whether it be teaching mathematics or teaching students to make positive life choices. The difference that exists between teaching and counselling is not in their defined objectives as much as in their process and methodology. Therefore, the functions of the teacher and the counsellor are complementary and not separate and independent. The necessity therefore for teachers and counsellors to establish a co-operative relationship based on equality is imperative.

In building a quality relationship with teachers, counsellors must learn to use the art of consultation and their training in interpersonal communications to ensure that their role, with its limitations and capabilities, is clearly understood. They must also learn to accept and regard teachers as co-professionals who have great knowledge, experience and insight into the needs of students. Teachers should be seen as a valuable resource from whom the counsellor can learn a great deal. Because teachers have much more contact time with students than counsellors have, teachers have a more consistent and long-term influence on them. Such a relationship reinforces the critical role of teachers and the importance of their input into the work of the counsellor. Counsellors need to be cognizant of this input and recognize that both teacher and counsellor play an equal and essential part in the educational endeavors of the students.

Teachers should also see counsellors as co-professionals with specialized knowledge in human behavior, adolescent and child psychology, etc. Teachers can use the counsellor's specialized knowledge when working with students in their classes. Counsellors can be available to teachers as resource persons to help them develop added competencies in such areas as counselling methodology, student appraisal procedures, etc. Together, the teacher and counsellor can more effectively assist students in their day-to-day struggle with the educative process (Adam, 1968).

By establishing relationships based on equality and trust, both counsellors and teachers can go beyond simply giving individual assistance to students. Together they can also get involved in actually modifying the learning environment in which students live. Both counsellors and teachers have the responsibility to use each other's expertise, indeed the expertise of all human resources available to them, in order to help their clients and students obtain the most from a successful counselling/educational program.

Counsellor/Administrator Relationship

In their study of middle school counsellors, Remly and Albright (1988) found that administrators were evenly split on their expectations (perceptions) of the role of the counsellor. While half the administrators saw the role of counsellors as specifically working with students and consulting with teachers and parents, an equal number saw this role combined with the additional role of administrator or semi-administrator. This is a significant finding, since it shows a still prevailing mind-set by many administrators that counsellors, because of their flexible schedule and non-attachment to a classroom, are free to be quasi-administrators or another vice-principal. Many school administrators see the school counsellor as a Jack (Jill)-of-all-trades. It is this type of thinking that prompts school administrators to delegate to the school counsellor such tasks as curriculum planning, student attendance, schedule making, discipline, substitute teaching, etc. This puts the school counsellor in a very untenable position. If one is hired to do a specific job and is then loaded down with a lot of seemingly unrelated tasks, one will be unable to perform effectively the specific assignments of that job for which one is hired. In addition, many of these tasks can easily create a conflict of interest for the counsellor. For example, as discussed earlier, the role of disciplinarian/informant is not compatible with the primary role of counsellor. What reasons exist to explain these role expectations of counsellors by administrators? Podemski and Childer (1988) believe that the unique talents and abilities of the counsellor have been overlooked and underused and suggest different reasons for this belief. Two of these are of particular significance:

1. Counsellors have been asked to assume quasi-administrative duties such as scheduling, advisement and discipline. As a result, counsellors often have little time to help students with personal, social and career concerns.
2. Counselling personnel often stereotype principals and instructional supervisors as being insensitive to the needs of the counselling/guidance program and staff. This perception may limit the quantity and quality of communication (regarding their role) counsellors initiate with principals and supervisors.

These two statements make one point very clear, namely, that counsellors and administrators do not always communicate adequately as to how the counsellor can best contribute to the school. Such a lack of communication results in role confusion, and leads to underuse or misuse of the unique skills and abilities of the counsellor.

In their efforts to differentiate the counsellor and administrator role, counsellors and administrators can benefit from an understanding of Podemski and Childer's (1988) list of six major "organizational common" factors between counsellor and administrator, which they see as contributing to such role confusion.

1. Interaction with all School Reference Groups

Counsellors interact with students, teachers, administrators, parents and community groups. Other than the counsellor, probably only the principal has the opportunity to interact regularly with all of these relevant school reference groups.

2. System Perspective

Counsellors are in an organizational position to view the school from a systems perspective, rather than a classroom or grade level perspective. As a result, they have information about the total school.

3. Staff Authority

Counsellors have staff rather than line authority. Because staff authority is based upon specialized knowledge and skills, the recommendations of the counsellor tend to be viewed by school personnel as serving the good of the organization rather than as being self-serving.

4. Confidentiality of Information

The confidential status of the counsellor is unquestioned and is perhaps the most singular advantage of the role. Because this privilege is universally recognized and respected by all reference groups in the school, the counsellor is often sought out for advice or counsel. Thus, the counsellor is in an excellent position to sense organizational problems and bring them to the attention of those who can develop solutions. In performing this function, the counsellor must ensure that the confidence of individuals is maintained while the organizational problem itself is identified and addressed

5. Access to Data

The position gives the counsellor access to a variety of data. Through data collection and analysis, the counsellor can access organizational needs, sense problems and facilitate change.

6. Flexible Schedule

Compared to classroom teachers, counsellors have a fairly flexible schedule. This flexibility enables counsellors to order priorities and to direct their energy according to the perceived needs of clients (students) and of the organization.

The above principles should be thoroughly discussed by school counsellors and administrators before the counsellor accepts a position on staff. Each should become aware of their similarities and differences and reach some consensus on how their roles can actually complement each other (Hannaford, 1987). Having accepted a position, the counsellor should spend time with administrators discussing productive ways in which to best provide services to the students. Such discussions between counsellor and administrator should be ongoing. Regular meetings throughout the year will provide for continuous progress and will help develop a clear understanding of what is happening, what is needed, and what actions or strategies should be implemented. Such continuous communication can do much to help avoid or correct any role confusion.

Establishing open and honest working relationships with teachers and administrators is but one of the many challenges facing school counsellors. However, it is one of the most important challenges and has an enormous influence on the success of the total counselling practice in the school.

There is a realization within the counselling profession that there exists, specifically in schools and other such institutions, a need for open and positive relationships between the various professionals working within these institutions. It is incumbent on all professionals who work in these institutions that they be ever cognizant of their primary goal, which is to meet the needs of clients within these institutions.

References

Adams, J. F. (1968). *Counselling and guidance: A summary view*. New York: MacMillan Company.

Adler, A. (1955). *The practise and theory of individual psychology*. London: Routledge and Kegan.

Alexander, F. (1963). *Fundamentals of psychoanalysis*. New York: W.W. Norton.

Allison, D. (1994). *The name of the phoenix, or where Greenfield (and Griffiths) went wrong*. Paper presented at the 8th International Intervisitation Program in Educational Administration, Toronto.

American Psychological Association (1956). "Counselling psychology as a specialty." *American Psychologist, 11*, 282-28.

Arbuckle, D.S. (1965). *Counselling: Philosophy, theory and practice*. Boston: Allyn & Bacon.

Argyris, C. (1982). *Reasoning, learning, and action*. San Francisco: Jossey-Bass.

Argyris, C. & Schon, D.A. (1974). *Theory in practice: Increasing professional effectiveness*. San Francisco: Jossey-Bass.

Aronowitz, S. & Giroux, H.A. (1991). *Post modern education*. Minneapolis: University of Minnesota Press.

Ashby, W.R. (1963). *An introduction to cybernetics*. New York: John Wiley & Sons.

Auserwald, E. (1966). *Interdisciplinary versus ecological approach*. Paper presented at the American Psychiatric Association, May 1966.

Avis, J. (1982). "Counseling: Issues and challenges." *Education and Urban Society, 15*, 70-87.

Ball, R.A (1978). "Sociology and general systems theory." *The American Sociologist, 13*, 65-62.

Barth, R.S. (1990). *Improving schools from within*. San Francisco: Jossey-Bass.

Baylis, F. (1993). "Therapist-patient sexual contact: A non consensual, inherently harmful activity." *Canadian Journal of Psychiatry*. Vol. 38. pp. 502-506.

Beck, N. (1992). *Shifting gears: Thriving in the new economy*. Toronto: Harper and Collins.

Beck, N. (1995). *Accelerate: Growing in the new economy*. Toronto: Harper and Collins.

Berger, R.L. & Luckman, T. (1966). *The social construction of reality*. New York: Doubleday.

Berne, E. (1967). *Games people play*. New York: Grove Press.

Berquist, W. (1993). *The post modern organization: Mastering the art of irreversible change*. San Francisco: Jossey-Bass.

Bertalanffy, L. Von. (1968). *General systems theory*. New York: George Braziller.

Beyer, R. & Liston, D. (1992). "Discourse or moral action? A critique of post modernism." *Educational Theory*, 42(4).

Blacker, F. (1992). "Formative context and activity systems: Post modern approaches to the management of change." In M. Reed and M. Hughes (eds) *Rethinking organizations: New directions in organization theory and analysis.* London: Sage.

Blackham, H.S. (1974). Ethical standards in counselling. London: Bedford Press. Cited in Cooper, G.F. (1992).

Blocher, D.H. (1965). "Issues in counselling: Elusive and illusional." *Personal and Guidance Journal*, 43, 796-8.

Blocher, D.H. (1966). *Developmental counselling.* New York: Ronald Press.

Blocher, D.H., Dustin, J. & Dugan W.E. (1971). *Guidance systems.* New York: Ronald Press.

Block, P. (1993). *Stewardship.* San Francisco: Berrett-Koehler.

Blum, M.L. & Bolinsky, B. (1962). *Counselling and psychotherapy.* Englewood Cliffs: Prentice Hall.

Boehner, P. (1957). *Ockham-philosophic writings.* Toronto. Thomas Nelson and Sons.

Bohm, D. (1980). *Wholeness and the implicate order.* London: Ark.

Bohm, D. (1985). *Unfolding meaning: A weekend of dialogue with David Bohm.* London: Ark.

Bolman, L. & Deal, T. (1991). *Reframing organizations: Artistry, choice and leadership.* San Franciso: Jossey-Bass.

Bond, T. (1992). "Ethical issues in counselling in education." *British Journal of Guidance and Counselling*, 20(1).

Boulding, K.E. (1956). "General systems theory – the skeleton of science." *Management Science*, 2.

Brammer, L.M. & Shostrum, E.L. (1968). *Therapeutic psychology.* (2nd ed.) New Jersey: Prentice Hall.

Bray, J.H., Shepherd, J.N. & Hays, J.R. (1985). "Legal and ethical issues in informed consent to psychotherapy." *American Journal of Family Therapy*, 12, 50-60.

Broverman, I. et al. (1970). "Sex role stereotypes and clinical judgments of mental health." *Journal of Consulting Psychology*, 34, 1-7.

Buczek, T. (1981). "Biases in counselling: Counsellor retention of concerns of a female and male client." *Journal of Counselling Psychology*, 28, 13-21. Cited in Robinson, B. and Page, S. (1988).

Calas, M. & Smircich, L. (1992). "Re-writing gender into organizational theorizing: Directions from feminist perspectives." In M. Reed & M. Hughes (Eds.), *Rethinking organization: New directions in organizational theory and analysis* (pp. 227-2 3). London: Sage.

Calderhead, J. (1989). "Reflective teaching and teacher education." *Teaching and Teacher Education*, 5(1), 43-51.

Caldwell, B. & Spinks, J. (1992). *The self-managing school.* London: Sage.

Canadian Guidance & Counselling Association (1988). *An ethical standards casebook.* Scarborough: Nelson Canada.

Canadian Guidance and Counselling Association (1989). *Guidelines for ethical behaviour.* Ottawa: W.E. Schulz

Canadian Psychological Association (1988). *Canadian code of ethics for psychologists*. Quebec: Canadian Psychological Association.

Carroll, L. (1946). *Alice's adventures in wonderland*. New York: Random House.

Chewning, R. (1984). *Business ethics in a changing culture*. Boston: Prentice-Hall.

Clegg, S.R. (1990). *Modern organizations: Organization studies in the post modern world*. London: Sage.

Clift, R.T., Houston, W.R. & Pugach, M.C. (1990) (Eds.). *Encouraging reflective practice in education: Analysis of issues and programs*. Teachers' College: Columbia University.

Cohen, K. (1992). "Some legal issues in counselling and psychotherapy." *British Journal of Guidance and Counselling, 20*(1).

Collaborative Action Working Group on Counselling (1988). *Report of the collaborative action working group on counselling*. First Ministers Conference (1986).

Collier, Helen (1982). *Counselling women – a guide for therapists*. New York: The Free Press.

Conley, D. (1993). *Roadmap to restructuring: policies, practices and emerging visions of schooling*. Eugene, OR: ERIC Clearinghouse.

Cook, D.R. (1971). *Guidance for education in revolution*. Boston: Allyn & Bacon.

Cook, Ellen Piel (1993). "The gendered context of life: Implications for women's and men's career life plans." *The Career Development Quarterly, 41*.

Cooper, G.F. (1992). "Ethical issues in counselling and psychotherapy: The background." *British Journal of Guidance and Counselling, 20*(1).

Cooper, J.M. et al. (1994). *Classroom teaching skills*. Toronto: D.C. Heath and Company.

Corey, C. et al. (1988). *Group techniques*. California. Brooks Cole.

Corsini, R.J. (1973). *Current psychotherapies*. Illinois: Peacock Publishing.

Cottone, R. (1991). "Counsellor roles according to two counselling world views." *Journal of Counselling and Development, 69* (5).

Cramer, S.H. et al. (1970). *Research and the school counsellor*. Boston: Houghton Mifflin.

Cruickshank, D. (1985). "Uses and benefits of reflective teaching." *Delta Kappan, 66*, 704-706.

Cruickshank, D.R. & Applegate, J. (1981). "Reflective teaching as strategy for teacher growth." *Educational Leadership, 38*(7), 553-554.

Culley, S. (1991). *Integrative counselling skills*. London: Sage.

Cunningham, W. & Gresso, D. (1993). *Cultural leadership*. Boston: Allyn & Bacon.

Curry, B.K. (1992). *Instituting enduring innovations: Achieving continuity of change in higher education*. ASHE-ERIC Higher Education Report No.7. Washington, DC: The George Washington University School or Education and Human Development.

Daindow, S. & Bailey, C. (1988). *Developing skills with people*. NY: John Wiley.

Daniluk, J.C. (1989). "The process of counselling: A spiral model." *Canadian Journal of Counselling, 23*(4).

Davidson, M. (1988). *Uncommon sense: Life and thought of Ludwig von Bertalanffy*. Boston: Houghton Mifflin.

Davis, R.T. & Ritchie, M. (1993). "Confidentiality and the school counsellor: A challenge for the 1990s." *The School Counsellor 41*, 23-30.

Day, C. (1993). "Reflection: A necessary but not sufficient condition for professional Development." *British Education Research Journal, 19*(1), 83-93.

Denkowski, K.M. & Denkowski, G.C. (1982). Client-counsellor confidentiality: An update of rationale, legal status and implications. *The Personnel and Guidance Journal, 60*, 371-375.

Dewey, J. (1938). *Experience and education.* New York: Collier-Macmillan.

Dinkmeyer, D. (1979). *Adlerian counselling and psychotherapy.* Monterey: Brooks/Cole Publishing Co.

Dixon, D. & Glover, J. (1985). *Counselling – a problem solving approach.* NY: John Wiley.

Doyle, C., Kennedy, W., Rose, A. & Singh, A. (1995). *Towards building a reflective and critical internship program (RCIP) model.* A monograph. Memorial University of Nfld.

Driekurs, R. (1968). *Psychology in the classroom.* NewYork: Harper & Row.

Drucker, P. (1989). *The new realities.* New York: Harper-Collins.

Drucker, P. (1995). *Managing in a time of great change.* New York: Truman Tolby Books.

Dryden, W. (1991). *Dryden on counselling.* Sessional papers. London: Whurr

Dryden, W. & Feltham, C. (1992). *Brief counselling.* Philadelphia: Open University Press.

Duska, R. (1993). "Aristotle: A premodern-post modern?" *Business Ethics Quarterly, 3*(3), 227-249.

Eagan, G. (1994). *The skilled helper* (5th ed). California: Brooks/Cole.

Ehrhart, J.K. & Sandler, B.R. (1987). *Looking for more than a few good women in traditional male fields.* Washington, D.C.: Association of American Colleges.

Ellis, A. (1962). *Reason and emotion in psychotherapy.* New York: Lyle Stuart.

English, H.B. & English, A.C. (1958). *A comprehensive dictionary of psychological and psychiatric terms.* New York: McKay

Everstine, L. et al. (1980). "Privacy and confidentiality in psychotherapy." *American Psychologist, 35*, 828-840.

Feiman-Nemser, S. (1990). "Teacher preparation: Structural and conceptual alternatives." In Houston, W.R., Haberman, M. & Sikula, J. (1990), *Handbook of Research on Teacher Education.* New York: Macmillan Publishing Company.

Ferry, L. & Renaut, A. (1990). "French philosophers of the sixties." In Rosenau, P. (1992) *Post modernism and the social sciences.* New Jersey. Princeton University Press.

Fine, R. (1973). "Psychoanalysis." In Corsini, R. (ed) *Current psychotherapies.* Chicago: Peacock.

Foster, W. (1986). *Paradigms and promises: New approaches for educational administration.* Buffalo, NY: Promethus

Foucault, M. (1980). *Power/knowledge.* New York: Pantheon Books.

Foucault, M. (1988). "The political technology of individuals." In Martin, L., Gutman, H. & Huttan, P. (Eds.). *Technologies of self: A seminar with M. Focault.* Amherst: University of Massachusetts Press.

Frankl, V. (1955). *The doctor and the soul*. New York: Knopf.

Frankl, V. (1963). *Man's search for meaning*. New York: Washington Square Press.

Frankl, V. (1969). *The will to meaning: Foundations and applications of logotherapy*. New York: New American Library.

Freud, S. (1920). *A general introduction to psychoanalysis*. New York: Boni and Liveright

Fromme, E. (1947). *Man for himself*. New York: Holt, Rinehart & Winston.

Fullan, M.G. (1993). *Change forces: Probing the depths of educational reform*. London: Falmer.

Fullan, M. & Hargreaves, A. (1991). *What's worth fighting for? Working together for your school*. Toronto: Ontario Teacher's Federation.

Garner, H.H. (1970). *Psychotherapy confrontation problem solving technique*. St. Louis: Guen.

Gazda, G. (1971). *Group counselling: A developmental approach*. Boston: Allyn & Bacon.

Gazda, G. (1977). *Human relations development: A manual for educators*. (2nd ed). Boston: Allyn & Bacon.

Gehring, D. (1982). "The counsellors duty to warn." *Personnel and Guidance Journal, 60*, 208-210.

George, R.L. & Dustin, D. (1988). *Group counselling: Theory and practice*. California: Prentice-Hall.

George, R. & Cristiani, T. (1990). *Counselling: Theory and practice*. Englewood Cliffs, NJ: Prentice Hall.

Gergen, K. (1992). "Organization theory in the post modern era." In Reed, M. and Hughes, M. (eds.), *Rethinking organization theory and analysis*. London: Sage.

Gergen, K. (1990). "Affect and organization in the post modern society." In Srivastva, S. & Cooperrider, D. (eds). *Appreciative management and leadership: The power of positive thought and action in organizations*. San Francisco: Jossey Bassey

Gibb, J. (1968). "The counsellor as a role free person." In Parker, C. (Ed.). *Counselling theory and counsellor education*. Boston: Houghton Mifflin.

Giroux, H. (1988). "Post modernism and the discourse of educational criticism." *Journal of Education, 170*(3), 3-18.

Glanz, E.G. (1974). *Guidance foundations, principles and techniques*. Boston: Allyn & Bacon.

Gleick, J. (1987). *Chaos: Making a new science*. Harmondsworth: Penguin Books.

Glickman, C. (1992). "The essence of school renewal: The prose has begun." *Educational Leadership, 50*(1), 24-27.

Glosoff, H. & Koprowicz, C. (1990). "Children achieving potential: An introduction to elementary school counseling and state level policies." In Thomson, C. & Rudolph, L. *Counselling Children* (1996). Brooks/Cole Publishing Company.

Goldner, V. (1985). "Feminism and family therapy." *Family Process, 24*, 13-47.

Goodman, J. (1983). "How to get more mileage out of your life: Making sense of humour then serving it." In McGhee, P. and Goldstein, J. (pp. 1-21). *Handbook of Human Resources*. New York: Springer-Verlag.

Gore, J.M. & Zeichner, K.M. (1991). "Action research and reflective teaching in preservice teacher education: A case study from the United States." *Teaching and Teacher Education*, 7(2), 119-136.

Grau, U., Moller, J. & Gunnarsson, J. (1988). "A new concept in counselling." *Applied Psychology*, 37(1).

Greene, M. (1986). "Reflection and passion in teaching." *Journal of Curriculum and Supervision*, 2(6), 68-81.

Green, R. (1993). "Business ethics as a post modern phenomenon." *Business Ethics Quarterly*, 3(3), 219-225.

Griffiths, D. (1994). *After Greenfield-what?* A paper presented at the 8th International Intervisitation Program in Educational Administration, Toronto.

Griggs, S. (1994). *Learning styled counselling: Counselling and student services*. University of North Carolina: Clearinghouse.

Gross, D. & Robinson, E. (1985). "Ethics: The neglected issue in consultation." *Journal of Counselling and Development*, 64(1).

Gross, D. & Robinson, E. (1987). "Ethics, violence and counselling: Hear no evil, see no evil, speak no evil?" *Journal of Counselling and Development*, 65, 340-344.

Guiness, O. (1993). *The American hour*. New York: The Free Press.

Gustad, J.W. (1957). "The evaluation interview: Vocational counselling." *Personal and Guidance Journal*, 36, 242-250.

Gysbers, N.C. & Moore, E.J. (1981). *Improving guidance programs*. Englewood Cliffs, NJ: Prentice Hall.

Habermas, J. (1975). *The legitimate crisis*. Translated by T. McCarthy. Boston: Beacon.

Hahn, M. & MacLean, M. (1955). *Counselling psychology*. New York: McGraw-Hill.

Handal, G. & Louvas, P. (1987). *Promoting reflective teaching: Supervision in practice*. Philadelphia: Open University Press.

Hannaford, M.J. (1987). "Balancing the counselling program to meet school needs." *NASSP Bulletin*, 71, 3-4, 6-9.

Hansen, D.A. (1969). *Explorations in sociology and counselling*. New York: Houghton Mifflin.

Hansen, J., Stevic, R. & Warner, R. (1986). *Counselling: Theory and process*. (4th ed.) Newton: Allyn & Bacon.

Hansford, S. (1988). "Selected trends in the economic status of American women (1900-1986): Implications for employment counsellors." *Journal of Employment Counselling*, 25.

Hare-Mustin, R.T. (1994). "Discourses in the mirrored room: A post modern analysis of therapy." *Family Process*, 33, 19-35.

Hargreaves, A. (1994). *Changing teachers, changing times: Teachers work and culture in the post modern age*. Toronto: OISE Press

Hassard, J. (1993). "Post modernism and organizational analysis: An overview." In Hassard, J. & Parker, M. (Eds.). *Post modernism and Organizations* (pp. 1-23). London: Sage.

Hassard, J. (1996). "Exploring the terrain of modernism and post modernism in organization theory." In Boje, D. et al. (1996), *Post modern management and organization theory*. Sage Publications.

Herlihy, B. & Corey, G. (1992). *Dual relationships in counselling.* Alexandria, VA: American Association for Counselling and Development.

Herlihy, B. & Sheeley, V. (1988). "Counsellor liability and the duty to warn: Selected cases statutory trends, and implications for practice." *Counsellor Education and Supervision, 27*, 203-215.

Hiebert, B. & Uhlemann, M. (1993). "Counselling psychology: Development, identity and issues." In Dobson, K. & Dobson, D. (Eds). *Professional psychology in Canada.* Seattle: Hogrefe & Huber Publishers.

Hollis, J. & Hollis, L. (1965). *Organizing for effective guidance.* Chicago: Science Research Associates Inc.

Hopkins-Best, M. (1987). "The effect of students' sex and disability on counsellors' agreement with post-secondary career goals." *The School Counsellor, 35(1).*

Horney, K. (1945). *Our inner conflicts.* New York: Norton.

Houston, W.R. et al. (1990). *A study of induction of 3 first year teachers and their mentors.* (Eric Document No. 338588.)

Hoyt, K. (1962). "Guidance: A constellation of services." *The Personal and Guidance Journal, 40*, 690-697.

Hoyt, K.B. (1989). "The career status of women and minority persons: A 20 year retrospective." *The Career Development Quarterly, 37*, 202-212.

Huey, W.C. (1986). "Ethical concerns in school counselling." *Journal of Counselling and Development, 64(5).*

Hultgren, F.H. (1987). "The student teacher as a person: Reflection on pedagogy and being." *Phenomenology and Pedagogy, 5(1),* 35-50

Jencks, C. (1987). *Post-modernism: The new classicism in art and architecture.* New York: Rizzoli

Johnson, D.L. (1990). "Developing family environment with families." In Kaslow, F. (Ed) *Voices in family psychology.* Newbury Park: Sage Publications.

Jones, A.J. (1963). *Principles of guidance.* New York: McGraw-Hill.

Juhnke, G.A. (1994). "Teaching suicide risk assessment to counsellor education students." *Counsellor Education and Supervision, 34*, 52-57.

Kain, C. (1988). "To breach or not to breach: is the question? A response to Gray and Harding." *Journal of Counselling and Development, 66*, 224-225.

Kanfer, F.H. & Goldstein, A.P. (1986). *Helping people change.* (3rd. ed.) New York: Pergamon Press.

Kaslow, F. and Associates (1979). *Supervision, consultation and staff training in the helping professions.* San Francisco. Jossey-Bass Publishers.

Kaslow, F. (1990). *Voices in family psychology.* Newbury Park: Sage.

Katz, M. (1987). "The rationale for a career guidance workbook." *Career Development Quarterly, 36.*

Kelly, G. (1955). *The psychology of personal constructs.* NY: Norton.

Kemmis, S. & McTaggart, R. (1988). *The action research planner.* Melbourne: Deakin University.

Kennedy, W.J. & Doyle, C. (1995). *Perceptions of internship evaluation.* St. John's, Newfoundland: Memorial University of Newfoundland.

Kerr, W. (1967). *Tragedy and comedy.* London. Bodley Head.

Kimmis, S. (1985). "Action research and the politics of reflection." In Boud, D., Keough, R. & Walker, D. (Ed.). *Reflection: Turning experience into learning*. London: Kogan Page.

Kitchener, K.S. (1985). "Ethical principles and ethical decisions in student affairs." In Canon, H.J. & Brown, R.D. (Ed.). *Applied ethics in student services: New directions for student services*. San Francisco: Jossey Bass.

Kolb, D. (1984). *Experimental learning*. New Jersey: Prentice Hall.

Kolb, D. (1990). *Post modern sophisitications: Philosophy, architecture and tradition*. Chicago: University of Chicago.

Kuhlman, T. (1984). *Humour and psychotherapy*. Illinois: Dow-Jones-Irwin.

Kuhn, D. (1990). *The structure of scientific revolutions*. Chicago: University of Chicago.

Kushel, G. (1967). *Discord in teacher-counsellor relations: Cases from the teacher's view*. New Jersey: Prentice-Hall.

Kutzik, A.J. (1979). "The medical field." In Kaslow, F. & Associates (1979), *Supervision, consultation and staff training in the helping professions*. San Francisco. Jossey-Bass Publishers.

Laidlaw, T. & Malmo, C. (1991). "Feminist therapy." *Canadian Journal of Counselling*, 25(4), 392-406.

Lamb, D. et al. (1989). "Applying Tarasoff to AIDS-related psychotherapy issues." *Professional Psychology: Research and Practice*, 20, 37-43.

Lash, S. (1990). *Sociology of Post Modernism*. London: Routledge.

Lash, S. & Ury, J. (1987). *The end of organized capitalism*. Cambridge: Polity.

Leithwood, K. (1992). "The move toward transformational leadership." *Educational Leadership*, 45(5), 4-8.

Leone, R.E. (1986). "Life after laughter: One perspective." *School Guidance & Counselling*, 139-142.

Lessing, D. (1986). *Prisons we choose to live inside*. Montreal: CBC.

Levine, H. (1980). "New directions for girls and women: A look at the condition of women in society and feminist counselling." *Counselling: Challenge of the Eighties*. St John's: CGCA Conference.

Lewis, J.A. (1992). "Gender sensitivity and family empowerment." *Topics in Family Psychology and Counselling*, 1-4, 1-7.

Ligon, M.G. & McDaniel, S.W. (1970). *The teacher's role in counselling*. New Jersey: Prentice-Hall Inc.

Linstead, S. (1993). "Deconstruction in the study of organizations." In Hassard, J. & Parker, M. (eds). *Post modernism and organizations*. London: Sage.

Luepnitz, D.A. (1988). *The family interpreted: Feminist theory in clinical practice*. New York: Basic Books.

Lusterman, D.D. (1988). "Family therapy and schools: An ecosystemic approach." *Family Therapy Today*, 3(7), 1-3.

Lynch, S.K. (1993). "Balancing confidentiality and the duty to protect." *Journal of College Student Development*, 34, 148-153.

Lyotard, J. (1993). *The post modern explained*. Minneapolis: University of Minnesota.

Lyotard, J. (1984). *The post modern condition*. Minneapolis: University of Minnesota.

Mahler, C.A. (1969). *Group counselling in schools.* Boston: Houghton Mifflin.

Marx, K (1984). "The poverty of philosophy." Cited in Gill, G., Post structuralism as idealogy. *Arena, 69,* 60-69.

Maslow, A. (1968). *Towards a psychology of being.* New York: Van Nostrand.

Maslow, A. (1970). *Motivation and personality.* New York. Harper and Rowe.

May, R., Angel, E. & Ellenberger, H. (1958). *Existence: A new dimension in psychiatry and psychology.* New York: Basic Books.

McCarthy, M.M. & Sorenson, G. (1993). "School counsellors and consultants: Legal duties and liabilities." *Journal of Counselling and Development,* Vol 17.

McCully, H. (1962). "The school counsellor strategy for professionalization." *The Personal and Guidance Journal, 40,* 681-689.

Meltzoff, J. & Kornreich, M. (1970). "Research in psychotherapy." Cited in Smith, M. et al. (1980), *The benefits of psychotherapy.* John Hopkins University Press, Baltimore, p. 56.

Miller, D.J. & Thelen, M.H. (1986). "Knowledge and beliefs about confidentiality in psychotherapy." *Professional Psychology: Research and Practice, 17,* 15-19.

Morreall, J. (1993). *Taking laughter seriously.* Albany: State University of New York.

Morse, K.L. (1990). "A uniform testimonial privilege for mental health professionals." *Ohio State Law Journal, 51,* p. 741-757.

Mower, O.H. (1960). "Sin the lesser of two evils." *American Psychologist, 15,* 301-304.

Murgatroyd, S. (1985). *Counselling and helping.* England: British Psychological Society.

Newfoundland and Labrador Federation of Labour (1982). *A presentation to the Newfoundland and Labrador Human Rights Commission.*

Nichols, W. & Everett, C. (1986). *Systemic family therapy: An integrative approach.* New York: Guilford

Ohmae, K. (1989). *The borderless world.* New York: Free Press.

Osterman, K.F. (1990). "Reflective practice: A new agenda for education." *Education and Urban Society, 22*(2), 133-152.

Parker, C. (1968). *Counselling theory and education.* Boston: Houghton Mifflin.

Parsons, F. (1908). *Choosing a vocation.* Boston: Houghton Mifflin Co.

Patterson, C.H. (1966). *Theories of counselling and psychotherapy.* New York: Harper & Row.

Patterson, C.H. (1959). *Counselling and psychotherapy: Theory and practice.* New York: Harper & Row.

Perls, F.S. (1969). *Gestalt therapy verbatim.* Lafeyette, CA: Real People Press.

Perry, W.J. (1961). "Relationship of psychotherapy and counselling." *Annals of New York Academy of Science, 63,* 396-407.

Podemski, R. & Childers, J. (1980). "The counsellor as change agent: An organizational analysis." *School Counsellor, 27,* 168-174.

Podemski, R. & Childers, J. (1986). "The school counsellor's role: Reexamination and revitalization." *Planning and Changing, 18,* 290-96.

Pope, K.S. & Vasquez, M. (1991). *Ethics in psychotherapy and counselling: A practical guide for psychologists.* San Francisco: Jossey-Bass.

Reamer, F.G. (1991). "AIDS, social work and the 'duty to protect'." *Social Work, 36*(1) 56-60.

Reisman, J.M. (1971). *Toward the integration of psychotherapy*. New York: Wiley.

Remly, T.P. & Albright, P.L. (1988). "Expectations for middle school counsellors: Views of students, teachers, principals, and parents." *School Counsellor, 35,* 290-296.

Rest, J.R. (1979). *Development in judging moral issues*. Minneapolis: University of Minnesota Press.

Rifkin, J. (1995). *The end of work*. NY: G.P. Putnam's Sons.

Robinson, A. & Page, S. (1988). "Gender role and future orientation in a Canadian university population." *Canadian Journal of Counselling, 22*(2), 91-101.

Rogers, C. (1961). *On becoming person*. Boston: Houghton Mifflin.

Rogers, C. (1951). *Client-centred therapy: Its current practice, implications and theory*. Boston: Houghton Mifflin

Rogers, C. (1942). *Counselling and psychotherapy*. Boston: Houghton Mifflin.

Rosenau, P.M. (1992). *Post-modernism and social sciences*. NJ: Princeton University Press.

Ross, D.D. (1989). "First steps in developing a reflective approach." *Journal of Teacher Education, 40*(2), 22-30.

Satir, V. (1964). *Conjoint family therapy: A guide to theory and technique*. Palo Alto: Science and Behaviour Books.

Satir, V. (1972). *Peoplemaking*. Palo Alto: Science and Behaviour Books.

Schon, D.A. (1983). *The reflective practitioner. How professionals think in action*. New York: Basic Books.

Schwitzgeable, R. & Schwitzgeable, R.K. (1980). *Law and psychological practice*. Toronto. Wiley.

Sexual Harassment Board. (1992). *University-wide procedures on sexual harassment complaints*. St. John's: Memorial University Press.

Sheeley, V.L. & Herlihy, B.L. (1989). "Privileged communication in school counselling." In Huey, W.C. & Rimley, T.P. (eds.), *Ethical and legal issues in school counselling*. Alexandria, VA: A.C.A.

Simmons, J.M., Sparks, G.M., Starko, A., Pasch, M., Colton, A. & Grinberg, J. (1989). *Exploring the structure of reflective pedagogical thinking in novice and expert teachers: The birth of a developmental taxonomy*. Paper presented at the Annual Conference of the American Educational Research Association, San Francisco, CA.

Sinclair, C. (1993). "Codes of ethics and standards of practice." In Dobsin, K. & Dobsin, D. (Eds.), *Professional psychology in Canada*. Toronto: Hogrefe & Huber.

Singer, E. (1965). *Concepts in psychotherapy*. New York: Random House.

Singh, A. (1994). Cross national consultation in international collaboration. *The Morning Watch*, (21)3-4, pp. 33-42. Memorial University Press.

Skinner, B.F. (1953). *Science and human behaviour*. New York: Macmillan.

Smyth, J.Q. (1987). *Educating teachers: Changing the nature of pedagogical knowledge*. London: Falmer Press.

Spencer, H. (1860). "The social organism." *Westminster Review, 73,* 90-121.

Spiegel-Keith, P. & Koocher, G.P. (1985). *Ethics in psychology: Professional standards and cases.* New York: Random House.

Srebalus, D., Marinelli, R. & Messing J. (1982). *Career development: Concepts and procedures.* Monterey: Brooks/Cole Co.

Stadler, H. & Paul, R. (1986). "Counsellor educator's preparation in ethics." *Journal of Counselling and Development,* 64(5), 328-330.

Stanard, R. & Hazler, R. (1995). "Legal and ethical implications of HIV and duty to warn for counsellors: Does Tarasoff apply?" *Journal of Counselling and Development,* 73, 397-400.

Steffler, B. & Grant, H. (1972). *Theories of counselling.* (2nd ed.) New York: McGraw-Hill.

Stein, R.H. (1990). *Ethical issues in counselling.* Buffalo, NY: Prometheus Books.

Stuart, R.B. (1980). *Helping couples change.* New York: The Guilford Press.

Sugarman, L. (1992). "Ethical issues in counselling at work." *British Journal of Guidance and Counselling,* 20(1).

Super, D. (1955). "Transition from vocational guidance to counselling psychology." In Whiteley, J. (1980), *The history of counselling psychology.* Brooks/Cole Publishing Company.

Szasz, T.S. (1960). "The myth of mental illness." *American Psychologist,* 15, 113-118.

Tarasoff vs. Reagents of University of California, 551 p. 2nd 334 (Cal. 1976).

Tenniel, J. (1936). *The complete works of Louis Carroll.* NY: Random House.

Thorne, B. & Dryden, W. (1993). *Counselling: Interdisciplinary perspectives.* Philadelphia: Open University Press.

Tompkins, L. & Melving, T. (1993). "Client privacy and the school counsellor: Privilege, ethics and employer policies." *The School Counsellor,* 40, 335-342.

Truax, C.B. & Mitchell, K.M. (1971). "Research on certain therapist interpersonal skills in relation to process and outcome." In Bergin, A.E. & Garfield, S.L. (Eds.), *Handbook of psychotherapy and behaviour change: An empirical analysis.* New York: John Wiley.

Tyler, L. (1958). "Theoretical principles underlying the counselling process." *Journal of Counselling Psychology,* 5, 3-10.

Tyler, L. (1969). *The work of the counsellor.* (3rd ed.), New York: Appleton Century Crofts

Van Manen, M.J. (1977). "Linking ways of being knowing with ways of being practical." *Curriculum Inquiry,* 6(3), 205-228.

Vance, F.L. & Volsky, T.C. (1962). "Counselling and psychotherapy: Split personality or twins?" *American Psychologist,* 15, 565-570.

Vandercreek, L. & Knapp, S. (1984). "Counsellor confidentiality and life endangering clients." *Counsellor Education and Supervision,* 24, pp. 51-57.

Vriend, J. (1985). *Counselling powers and passions.* Virginia: American Association for Counselling and Development.

Wagner, C.F. (1981). Model for assessment of disruptive adolescents. *Psychological Reports.*

Watzlawick, P., Beavin, J.H. & Jackson, D.D. (1967). *Pragmatics of human communication: A study of interactional patterns, pathologies, and paradoxes.* New York: Norton.

Wedell-Monnig, J. & Westerman, T. (1982). "Assessment of parent-child interaction in an early intervention program." *Journal for Special Educators, 18,* 56-63.

Weinrach, S. (1979). *Career counselling: Theoretical and practical perspectives.* New York: McGrath Hill.

White, M, & Epston, D. (1990). *Narrative means to therapeutic ends.* New York: W.W. Norton.

Whiteley, J.M. (1980). *The history of counselling psychology.* California: Brooks/Cole.

Whiteley, J. & Fretz, B. (1980). *The present and future of counselling psychology.* California: Brooks/Cole.

Wiggens, J. & Westlander, D. (1986). "Effectiveness related to personality and demographic characteristics of secondary school counsellors." *Counsellor Education and Supervision, 26,* 26-35.

Wolf, N. (1992). *The beauty myth.* Toronto: Random House.

Wrenn, G. (1966). "Birth and early childhood of a journal." In Whiteley J.M. (1980). *The history of counselling psychology.* California: Brooks/Cole Publishing Company.

Shertzer, B. & Stone, S.C. (1974). *Fundamentals of counselling.* (2nd ed.) Boston: Houghton Mifflin.

Young, I. (1986). "The ideal of community and the politics of difference." *Social Theory and Practice, 12.*

Zeichner, K. & Gore, M.J. (1990). "Teacher socialization." In Houston, W.R., Haberman, M. & Sikula, J., *Handbook of research on teacher education.* New York: Macmillan Publishing Company.

Zinger, D. (1985). *The functions and factors of humour in counselling.* Unpublished Masters of Education thesis in Educational Psychology. Manitoba: University of Manitoba.

Ziv, A. (1984). *Personality and sense of humour.* New York: Springer.

Zytowski, D.G. & Rosen, D.A. (1982). "The grand tour: 30 years of counselling psychology." *The Counselling Psychologist. 10*(1), 69-81.